DATE DUE

Demco, Inc. 38-293

Praise for Kyle Maynard and NO EXCUSES

"When I interviewed Kyle Maynard, he touched the hearts of more viewers than perhaps any other interview I've done. *No Excuses* is the book that Kyle Maynard fans, like me, have been waiting for. And let me tell you, it's terrific."

—**LARRY KING**, Host, CNN's *Larry King Live*

"*No Excuses* will really pump you up. As a champion weightlifter and wrestler, Kyle Maynard is the real deal. But as a champion human being, he is one of the most inspiring people I've ever met. I recommend *No Excuses* to everyone."

—**ARNOLD SCHWARZENEGGER**, Governor of California and former champion body builder

"Significant achievement occurs to those who have the courage to overcome disappointment and setbacks to pursue their dreams. This is an inspirational book about the perseverance of the human spirit. Let Kyle inspire you!"

—**TROY AIKMAN**, Former quarterback, Dallas Cowboys

"No one surpasses Kyle's strength of body and more important, his will. He's incredibly inspirational. It's a privilege to know him and his story."

—**GEORGE BODENHEIMER**, President, ESPN, Inc. and ABC Sports

"Kyle Maynard's inspirational story proves that with hard work, faith and desire, you can achieve your goals. Kyle's recognized as an athlete, but above all he's a role model to the human race."

—**JOHN SMOLTZ**, Atlanta Braves

"Greatness is measured in different ways, but only has one common denominator, finding a way to succeed. Kyle Maynard has done that by making *No Excuses*."

—**WAYNE GRETZKY**, Greatest hockey player of all time

"Kyle Maynard's inspirational story is about succeeding against odds that most of us can't imagine. How does Kyle do it? His title says it all: '*No Excuses*.' That's a habit we could all adopt from this great book, written by a highly successful young man."

—Stephen R. Covey, Author, *The 7 Habits of Highly Effective People & The 8th Habit: From Effectiveness to Greatness*

"We often measure the heart of a champion by his success. I believe a true champion is measured by how he overcomes adversity. Kyle Maynard embodies the true champion spirit and motivates me to be a better athlete and a better person."

—Randy Couture, Ultimate Fighting Championship's heavyweight champion

"I admire Kyle Maynard, both on and off the mat. His tenacity to attack and conquer life's obstacles is inspiring."

—Andy Roddick, Top-Ranked Tennis Pro and U.S. Open Champion

"Kyle Maynard is the epitome of what an athlete is meant to be. *No Excuses* exemplifies how one individual's heart, dedication, and desire can overcome all obstacles."

—Scott Stevens, NHL Defenseman, New Jersey Devils

"A gripping tale of athleticism and competition, and a moving, inspiring story of one man's indomitable spirit. I couldn't put it down!"

—Liz Vaccariello, Executive editor, *Fitness* magazine

"Athletes like Kyle Maynard are an inspiration to the athletes who compete in the National Junior Disabilities Championships. They can truly see 'THERE ARE NO LIMITS.'"

—Arleen Sand, NJDC, Wheelchair Sports Hall of Fame

"This courageous story will be required reading for all of my athletes."

—Cody Sanderson, Head Wrestling Coach, Utah Valley State, Two time All American (Iowa State) and Two time NCAA finalist

No Excuses

No Excuses

The True Story of a Congenital Amputee
Who Became a Champion in Wrestling and in Life

Kyle Maynard

Since 1947
REGNERY
PUBLISHING, INC.
An Eagle Publishing Company • Washington, DC

Library of Congress Cataloging-in-Publication Data

Maynard, Kyle, 1986–
  No excuses : the true story of a congenital amputee who became a champion in wrestling and in life / Kyle Maynard.
     p. cm.
  ISBN 0-89526-011-5
  1. Maynard, Kyle, 1986– 2. Wrestlers—United States—Biography. 3. Athletes with disabilities—United States—Biography. 4. Amputees—United States—Biography. I. Title.
  GV1196.M38A3 2005
  796.812'092—dc22

                        2005018554

Published in the United States by
Regnery Publishing, Inc.
One Massachusetts Avenue, NW
Washington, DC 20001
www.regnery.com

Distributed to the trade by
National Book Network
Lanham, MD 20706

Manufactured in the United States of America

Typeset in Adobe Minion 11.5/19

10 9 8 7 6 5 4 3 2 1

Books are available in quantity for promotional or premium use. Write to Director of Special Sales, Regnery Publishing, Inc., One Massachusetts Avenue NW, Washington, DC 20001, for information on discounts and terms or call (202) 216-0600.

Contents

Foreword

by Coach Cliff Ramos

The lady on the phone asked if her sixth grade son could get started in our youth wrestling program at Collins Hill High School in Suwanee, Georgia. Even though I am the high school coach, I spoke for the youth coaches and told her: "Sure, no problem." She told me her son had a physical condition I should be aware of first. I told her not to worry, our youth coaches would be able to handle it. She told me her son had very short stubs for arms, and small feet that gave him only stubs for legs.

So basically, she was telling me that her 11 year old son wanted to be a wrestler though he had practically no arms or legs. I guessed I paused for a few moments, because then she told me not to worry.

That night I met Kyle Maynard at our youth practice, and a seven year journey began that changed my life and the lives of millions. My first thought when I met Kyle in person was: "The poor kid, he wants to wrestle, but he won't really be able to, and if he does, he will never win a match." Well, seven years later Kyle was the varsity 103-pounder on my team, which in itself was quite an achievement. He went on to win 35 matches that year, he qualified for the state tournament in Georgia's largest classification, he won three matches at the state tournament, and came one match from placing in the top 8 in the Senior National Tournament.

Watching him wrestle and succeed almost defied physics. There were times I looked at Kyle in practice or in a match and say to myself: "That is impossible!" But Kyle Maynard is the impossible. All of his life, he has done what seems impossible to most people.

That is why his story is so much more than a teenage boy with physical limitations who manages to become a top flight athlete. Just spending ten minutes with Kyle and watching him carry out his normal daily activities can inspire you so deeply that it will actually change your outlook on life. Try using your elbows to do such things as writing, typing, dressing yourself, using forks and spoons, talking on a cell phone, or getting in a car and driving. Kyle can do these things and practically everything else that any able-bodied person can do, and usually better than most people, even though he doesn't have the luxury of elbows, and just a few inches of legs!

Perhaps the most inspiring thing about Kyle is his "No Excuses" attitude. In the seven-plus years I have known Kyle, I have never heard him utter one excuse for anything. There were times when I chewed Kyle out after a match because I thought he could have done better. Never did I hear anything like, "Well, you know, Coach, I hardly have any arms, and it was really hard for me to reach the guy's leg..."

There have been times in my personal life when I have thought about Kyle to help me through a situation. I have pictured him in my mind in the middle of a third set of a tough tennis match. I have seen him when I have contemplated taking it easy on my team at practice because I might not be feeling well. I have even thought about Kyle when I have done some very tedious tasks around the house. I have thought about Kyle in moments of crisis. In all of these instances, I have asked myself, "Would Kyle give up here? Would he try to find an easier way out?" Now that's inspiration.

And the big thing is, I am not alone. Over the last two years, Kyle has had the opportunity to meet thousands of people in person and millions through the media. So many people he has met have gone away feeling... different. They are humbled, they are inspired, they are often brought to tears, and they are changed.

My philosophy is simple: No Excuses!

CHAPTER 1 **No Excuses**

This moment could be the last. My career as a high school varsity
wrestler could be over. I was behind in points and desperate to
score a takedown against my opponent. Time was running out,
and the excruciating pain from my uncovered broken nose nearly
brought tears to my eyes.

But I knew I couldn't give up.

This was no ordinary match. This was the Georgia State
Wrestling Tournament. For years, I had dreamed about competing
here. The loser of this bout would go home without a medal, but I was
fighting for more than that.

My opponent came from my high school's bitter regional rival,
so we'd met before—sometimes I'd won, and sometimes I'd lost.

Before the match began, I'd watched him jumping rope across the hall, knowing that no matter what happened today, this would be the final match between us. And I knew this could be my last chance to take the mat as a high school wrestler.

I couldn't remember ever feeling more on edge before a match. My neck tingled, and my body was quivering from anticipation and adrenaline, the only thing keeping my joints from locking in place. The roar from inside the tournament arena was deafening, and among the thousands of screaming spectators, I could feel the emotion pouring out of my family, friends, teammates, and coaches.

It was my fifth match of the tournament. My body was exhausted from the first four matches, and the last two had gone to sudden-death overtime. I could not allow a wasted second. In order to defeat this opponent, I needed to take advantage of any opening, to summon up every last ounce of speed, strength, and determination I had left inside of me.

I knew in my heart I deserved to win the match. I had invested so much time and effort, so much sweat and passion, into preparing for this moment that preparation itself was now the source of my fear. I was never afraid of the hard work and dedication that wrestling demanded of me—instead, I was afraid of experiencing the heartbreak of defeat after all the relentless training that had brought me to this point. I was no stranger to that fear, but knowing this could be my final match made it more acute.

For seven years, I had trained with weights and wrestled hard. Seven years of experience were condensed into this one match. Now I had to plow my body into my rival; I had to dominate not just his muscles but his mind; I had to drive him to submit.

My wrestling coach, Cliff Ramos, and I had developed a strategy to beat this opponent. While I was stronger, we all knew this wrestler had the advantage of agility and speed. We analyzed and planned, coming up with dozens of tactics to use or avoid—but I knew that winning, as always, was ultimately a matter of desire.

I wanted to strip my opponent of his confidence. I knew I might look like the underdog, but I wanted him to feel that here, on this day, he was the one who had the odds stacked against him.

Everyone in the Macon Centreplex arena could see that I was physically different from my opponent. I was born with shortened arms and legs. My condition is called congenital amputation. I have arms that end at the elbows and legs that end at the knees.

Yet I still believe that everyone on the wrestling mat is an equal, competitors standing on even ground. Everyone learns the same rules, steps on the same scale to weigh-in, walks onto the same mat alone, and listens for the same referee's whistle to start the match. I knew from experience that a clever, well-trained, and determined wrestler could always beat a buff, but unprepared, opponent. The key is using every one of your God-given abilities, not just strength, to the utmost.

Since the age of eleven, I've had a passion for wrestling. I'm a competitor. I believe that anyone can conquer any obstacle if they truly want it more than anything else; if they are ardent in their work; and if they refuse to be stopped by any barrier.

I've met people who wonder why I wrestle. Am I attempting to prove something to the world? Am I trying to have people feel sorry for me? Or am I simply trying to make friends, to be the token member on the team? Some people can't see the truth—that regardless of my physical difference, I am as fierce a competitor on the inside as anyone can be. On my shoulder is a tattoo of a tiger; that's how I think of myself, and that's how I fight.

I am an athlete driven by competition. Without the sport of wrestling, I would not be where I am today. There are so many problems and difficulties that I will never have to endure because of the character I've developed through wrestling. It is my discipline and my passion.

On that day in Georgia, I knew it didn't matter how much I was afraid, how much I was in pain, or how impossible the situation appeared to me. I knew the obstacles. This was no different from the rest of my life. We all have challenges to face, and to overcome. No obstacle would keep me from accomplishing my dreams.

It was Dan Gable, one of the greatest wrestlers and coaches of all time, who said: "Once you've wrestled, everything else in life becomes easy." No phrase describes my life better.

I carried that truth with me that fateful day in Georgia as I walked toward the center circle to begin the third period with my shattered nose, my exhausted body, and what some see as my physical handicap. But none of that mattered to me. I had to win.

The referee signaled to the time keeper, blew the whistle, and we set off.

My philosophy is simple: No excuses.

Even though I was born with much shorter limbs than the average person, I know that I was not born to be an inferior individual. I was born to succeed, not to allow physical limitations to stand in the way of my dreams.

CHAPTER 2 **Firstborn**

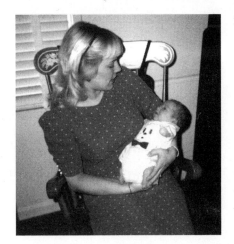

My parents were full of anticipation as they stepped into the obstetrician's office. There were so many hoops to jump through and things to experience—the questionnaire to answer, the nurse to sign them in, and the month-old magazines piled in stacks on tables. Waiting to be called into the back room seemed like an eternity.

For most parents, their unborn child is imagined perfectly, as the ideal combination of all the best facets of husband and wife mixed into one brand new person. In a loving family, the child represents the hopes and dreams for a next generation, sure to be smart, athletic, and beautiful. As you look at an ultrasound, you see the next Einstein, the next Jeter, Gretzky, or Jordan—or if it's two heartbeats, they're the new improved Venus and Serena.

For my parents, as there must be for any pregnancy, there was always a chance something could be out of order—so they made every effort to take all the appropriate precautions and followed every recommendation to ensure a healthy child. And they knew that the first pregnancy can be a stressful period, because so many things have the chance to go wrong.

I was their first born child, so these emotions weighed on my parents, Scott and Anita, all the more. But my mother's pregnancy had been completely normal. So as they prayed for a healthy and happy child that could grow up to fulfill their greatest dreams, sharing their emotions and their hopes for the future, they had no reason to worry. There were no problems. There was no reason for concern. The quiet fears were all drowned out by their eagerness to see their child for the first time.

Medical technology wasn't quite as advanced in those days as it is now. The clarity of today's ultrasound is a world away from the grainy pictures of a mere two decades ago. But the technology was still good enough to detect some of the things that might appear to be off—it could show doctors the signs of a difficult pregnancy, or something worse.

The nurse that day was kind and pleasant. She told my mother there was nothing to worry about—she was familiar with so many families who don't nurture their unborn children, either because they don't know any better, or because they don't care. Apathy is the main reason why so many children face dangerous problems, she said—and with all the effort my parents had put into being healthy and valuing this unborn life as an equal part of the family, my mother was doubtlessly carrying a perfectly healthy baby.

The nurse took the cold gel and slathered it across my mother's stomach, moving the ultrasound sensor methodically around her womb. She pointed out my head, abdomen, and beating heart for my parents on the blurry pictures. Then she began to make measurements to get an idea of my anticipated birth date. She measured the circumference of my head and midsection along with my spine.

A sudden look of confusion crossed the nurse's face, but she continued to move the sensor around to view different areas. The pulse from the ultrasound broke the deafening silence with a rhythmic beat.

My mother was fixated on the sensor moving across her abdomen, saying that it was making the baby kick—but my father noticed the bewildered look on the nurse's face. He looked at the monitor, trying to make out the blurry picture.

The nurse explained that she was having trouble finding the baby's femur. The leg measurements are how the doctors estimate the child's age, and sometimes the leg is tucked close to the torso. She decided to find a doctor, just to double check the pictures from the machine.

When the nurse excused herself from the room and stepped outside, my parents started to feel nervous. My father couldn't hear the conversation from inside the room, but he shared a concerned look with my mother.

"I'm sure everything is going to be okay," my father said. "This probably happens all the time, and we just don't know it."

Before my mother could reply, a radiologist stepped into the room. He greeted my parents cordially and started to analyze the reading from the ultrasound, looking closely at the ultrasound monitor. The room was dead silent as my parents watched him, chilly with the cold of the hospital air conditioner.

Finally, the radiologist's chair creaked as he turned and said, "I believe everything looks normal . . . You two have nothing to worry about."

The assistant couldn't find my limbs, but the radiologist said that, after a few minutes of searching, he had found something that looked like it might be a femur, or at least something they could measure to determine my age. The radiologist passed the sensor back to the nurse and asked her to see if this measurement seemed to match their estimates. It matched perfectly.

The radiologist reassured my parents that sometimes limbs can be hard to find, as they can get pushed behind the placenta, making it difficult to obtain a good image. Oftentimes it will even appear that something is missing when it isn't.

He'd seen this sort of thing happen on a number of occasions, and he'd never seen skewed ultrasound results end up as anything other than a normal birth. The chance of a child being born with minor limb dysfunction is one out of every few thousand, and the likelihood that the child would be born with all four limbs severely affected is one out of every few million.

The radiologist had a lengthy conversation with my parents, explaining the situation. He told them in nearly all cases where a child is born with a serious birth defect, the ultrasound will detect it. He saw nothing in the ultrasound to be cause for worry. If they found something later, the doctor said, they could discuss other options.

"What other options?"

"Other options generally involve aborting the child surgically," the doctor said. "If there is a serious dismemberment in the child, then the likelihood that the child could have a normal life is drastically reduced. Instead of putting that burden on the parents to care for a physically challenged child, we generally recommend you abort."

"That's not an option for us. We would never consider it."

The doctor told my parents to go home and rest easy. With a child that is only seventeen weeks old, these things happen quite often. He said he was confident they had a perfectly healthy child.

"Don't waste your energy worrying about something that virtually never happens. Save it for when the child is born."

My parents thanked the radiologist for taking the time to analyze the ultrasound, and the nurse apologized for the false alarm. But when my parents left the office, they were both worried.

For the next five months, my mother had regular check-ups that never indicated anything would be wrong. They even had another ultrasound in the third trimester and found nothing wrong.

My parents' feelings of worry were gradually pushed away as they prepared for my arrival with hope and confidence.

They were shocked when I was born.

TRAUMA IN THE DELIVERY ROOM

It was a bright Sunday morning, March 23, 1986, when my mother felt the first delivery contractions. The abrupt pain was a clear sign that it was time to head to the hospital.

My parents lingered in the delivery room together. Walter Reed Army Medical Hospital was, at that time, the premier hospital in Washington D.C., and for my father—a military policeman—it was the obvious place to go.

My parents spent hours discussing their hopes for their child, still unaware of whether it would be a boy or a girl. My parents were young, only a year into their marriage, and still very excited with the newness of it all. They good-naturedly disagreed about how many children they wanted to have—my father wanting a small family, my mother wanting a large one.

They started to feel a little fatigued as hours passed by and the contractions continued. My mother's water still hadn't broken, and she had been in labor for more than twelve hours. An epidural was administered through an IV as the contractions moved closer together.

By late Monday morning the water still had not broken. The doctors at Walter Reed decided that it was time to break the water and give additional medicine to my mother to hasten the contractions. Two nurses and a pediatrician joined the family obstetrician in the delivery room as my mother's contractions intensified. It wouldn't be long now, they assured my parents.

At 12:13 PM on Monday March 24, 1986, I came into the world. I was facedown and tucked in the fetal position.

My father was at the bedside, gripping my mother's hand. He wasn't able to see my face or chest because I came out facing the ground. For a moment, everything appeared to be normal.

Then the obstetrician passed me to the pediatrician without saying a word to my parents. He took me over to the table inside the room and washed me down with his back turned to my mother and father. He gave me the standard Apgar test (the health checklist for every newborn) as if nothing was wrong, but something clearly was.

The excitement and relief at the birth of their firstborn quickly turned into strained confusion. No one in the room would make eye contact with them. My parents were both too scared to ask what the problem was as the pediatrician wrapped me in a blanket and passed me to a nurse—both immediately left the room and shut the door behind them.

The obstetrician knelt down to finish the delivery by stitching my mother. A thick cloud of fear loomed over the room. My parents were stunned and silent.

Eventually, the obstetrician stood up and said, "I need to check on some things right away with your son, but I should be back with him in a moment."

"So it's a boy?"

"Yes, Scott...but some tests need to be done to make sure every-thing is in order before you can see him," the doctor said. "I'll go and check on that now."

The pediatrician stepped back inside the delivery room and paced toward my parents as he stared down at the floor. He slowly lifted his head to speak.

"There are some problems with the baby."

He paused, as if trying to find the right words, before explaining: "He is missing most of his limbs. We did some preliminary tests to determine if he has all of the necessary internal organs to survive, and everything else seems fine."

"It appears as though he'll be all right, but we want to make sure before you see him."

The doctor left my parents alone inside the delivery room. They didn't know what to do—they were too shocked by what had happened, too scared of the unknown, and too confused by the entire situation. They felt as though the world had collapsed around them. My father looked into my mother's eyes, and both of them began to tear up out of sheer uncertainty.

The obstetrician looked at my parents and tried to speak. "I'm sorry...I'm sorry," was all he could manage to get out. He left to check on me in the intensive care unit.

My father glanced over at the IV running into a vein in my mother's arm and noticed that the tube had lost its fluid. He rolled her over towards her stomach to examine what happened and discovered that during all of the chaos of the delivery, the IV had somehow slipped out. The table and its sheets were soaked in blood from a large vein, the blood running all over her back.

My father screamed out for help. Nurses rushed into the room, shoved the IV back inside of my mother, and rushed to pump blood inside of her to replace what she had lost.

My father stumbled back and collapsed in a chair. He was sick to his stomach and felt almost faint from trauma. His newborn son was undergoing urgent tests for a problem that no one could explain to him. His wife nearly died from blood loss on the delivery room table. Nothing could have prepared him for this.

The fear of the unknown nearly overwhelmed my parents before they were even allowed to see me. It took them a moment to gather courage to see their firstborn child—hoping for the best, praying against the worst—when the pediatrician returned, carrying me wrapped inside a blanket. He had a look of sympathy on his face as he passed me to my parents.

My father looked down at me and beamed. With my head supported by his shoulder, he took his left hand and uncovered the blanket to see my missing limbs. He didn't grimace. For a moment, he was proud that my features already resembled his.

My mother sighed with joy as she said, "I can't believe he's so beautiful."

As they talked, my parents felt God was telling them that everything would be all right; that He wanted them to celebrate the birth of their firstborn son, that they should dispel fear and doubt. The shock and uncertainty were still there, but prayer and faith kept my parents from succumbing to pessimism or depression. Prayer kept my parents going in the worst moments, even though it did not deny anything or magically remove worry. It was a dialogue of emotion and faith that kept my parents as balanced as they could be under the circumstances.

A nurse returned shortly after to carry me away for more tests. I spent the next three days in the hospital away from my parents. Half of the time I was in the intensive care unit while my family had to wonder what else could go wrong. Three days gave them a long time to ponder the worst possibilities, and still no one could provide a definitive answer about why this had happened or what the consequences might be.

Thankfully, the support system of my extended family was already coming together to help out. My grandparents on my mother's side were visiting family in Tifton, Georgia when I was born. As soon as they heard about me, my grandmother and grandfather rushed to the Atlanta airport and headed to Washington D.C. They knew it would be close to a fifteen hour drive and couldn't stand the thought of their daughter and son-in-law being alone at such a time. My father's mother flew in from Michigan at the same time. When they arrived, they found my parents distraught, exhausted, and shell-shocked by the experience.

Social worker after social worker tried to comfort my father and mother, but failed—my parents were overcome by needless guilt, denial, anger, and resentment. I was still going through test after test at this point, but each test just meant another possible worry.

My parents and grandparents prayed for hours that I would survive the first few days of my life. No one apparently had any certainty about what would happen to me. There were only questions that couldn't be answered.

My father didn't know what to do. He had planned on leaving the service once his term was up in three weeks. He was going to attend college in the fall. But now, as a young father with little margin for financial difficulty, he faced an enormous burden—the prospect of a tidal wave of medical bills, treatment, and God knows what. His hopes of obtaining a college degree appeared to be crushed; he had no immediate potential for a steady job, but he needed to find one. Even then, how would he pay the bills? He had every reason to expect that I would be far more expensive in my needs than a normal child, and without a college education, my father feared he could not earn the money our family would need.

After the hospital released me, my parents had a follow-up visit with Dr. Charles Epps, a specialist who had experience with kids like me. He told my parents that my condition is technically called Quadramembral Phocomelia, a defect that has an unknown cause. Congenital amputation happens about once every two thousand births or so—but it usually affects just a finger, or toes, or an arm.

Dr. Epps told my parents that it was likely I would end up using a wheelchair to get around when I was older. He urged them not to let anyone amputate my feet, explaining that while it would be easier for my legs to fit prosthetics if they did so, I would likely never be able to walk with prosthetic legs. He also arranged for my parents and me to meet with another family, who had gone through this same ordeal eighteen months earlier.

Through prayer, my parents came to accept that they couldn't change what had happened. They couldn't make me the perfect child they had dreamed about. They could only accept the reality of it, lean on their family, and have faith that things would work out for the best. They prayed for guidance.

Three weeks later, we moved to Fort Wayne, Indiana, where my mother's parents lived. My parents knew they needed help to raise me and to bear the emotional and financial burdens of the coming months and years.

My parents focused on the fact that they had a responsibility to work together and try to give me the best and happiest life that I could possibly have. In the end, I was the firstborn son in my family—and nothing else mattered.

I look everyone straight in the eye, as an equal, as God created all of us. We are all created uniquely, but we are all equally precious in God's eyes. That's something I believe in my heart, that my faith and my family taught me over and over again.

CHAPTER 3 **Bouncing Baby Boy**

Even given my physical difference, the first year of my life progressed in much the same way as any other child's. Concerns about my physical wellbeing disappeared as I continued to live a healthy life: I sat up, crawled, and spoke on schedule for a normal baby boy.

But that feeling of normalcy changed drastically when I turned one. I could no longer keep up with the progress that other children my age made—they began to stand, walk and have more functional abilities with their hands, while I was stuck without any of that progress.

At the time, I didn't notice. But the people who cared for me did. No one knew whether I would ever be able to function on my own without constant assistance.

My family treated me with more love than a child could ever have asked for. They tried to help me with anything and everything. They helped me eat, dress, and use the bathroom—all well past the point when physically normal children began doing these things on their own.

As I grew up, we arranged contraptions using paperclips and lanyards so I could have something to grip as I learned to put on my clothes by myself. Until recently, I still had trouble with some issues— putting my socks on, zipping my pants—that my parents would help me with. But I've gotten better at these practical things over time.

When I was a kid, my mother and grandmother would feed me, since I didn't yet know how to pour, drink, or use silverware. I gained weight fast, because they didn't know when to stop feeding me, and I was too young to refuse anything. I relied on them for help in almost every aspect of my life.

This soon became a problem. My father noticed how I was becoming completely dependent on my family, and he knew that in the future, the world would not be tailored to my every need. He knew that I would have to live on my own someday, and he wanted me to be as self-sufficient as possible.

It became my dad's mission to prepare me for that moment, to do anything it took so I could be fully independent later on in my life.

My arms came together and I could hold things between them. Yet I never fed myself at all. I even refused to feed myself because I was so accustomed to everyone doing it for me.

My father was certain that I could use a prosthetic spoon to eat, or use my arms to pick up types of foods that didn't require silverware. So he finally reached the point where he demanded that everyone stop feeding me. He said that I would have to learn how to eat on my own, or I would starve.

Of course, my father's a loving and compassionate man—he never abandoned me or left me to waste away—but on the outside, to me, he was firm in his decision to stop all the help I was receiving until I started to take responsibility and become more independent.

For the first few years of my life people fed me because they thought they had to. Now I needed to do some of the work on my own. I needed to understand this was the way the world worked. If I was going to live a normal life, learning how to eat and dress myself was essential.

I fed myself from that point on. I learned how to drink and pour by squeezing the cup or bottle between my arms. I had a prosthetic device with a spoon that cupped onto my arm to swing the food into my mouth. We treated this device the way people treat training wheels on a bike, and hoped it wouldn't be necessary forever.

I used the prosthetic spoon for the next five years—it was a clumsy, but effective, tool. But after a few years, I started to leave the spoon all over the place; I'd leave it at restaurants and friends houses over and over again out of absentmindedness. So I decided, with the guidance of my parents, to learn to use regular silverware so that I wouldn't be dependent on having the spoon.

At first, I had a number of setbacks. I spilled food repeatedly when I tried to lift the regular silverware to my mouth. It took a long time to become comfortable with using normal forks and spoons to eat.

At long last I found a way to break through the barrier, and I invented a new way to balance the silverware on one of my arms and use the other arm to swing the food towards my mouth. I still use that method to this day, so I can eat just about any meal in any restaurant.

This obstacle was just the first of hundreds I had to overcome in order to pursue a normal life. Other children had to learn to eat, too—my learning process was just a little more complicated. I would encounter many more situations like that and did my best each time to overcome them by myself. In each case, I recognized that I was facing a unique difficulty, but that didn't mean it was an impossible one.

As things calmed down after we made the move to Indiana, my father decided to go to college and finish his education. My mother had to work in order to support the family, so she found work as a secretary. She abandoned her ambition to become a school teacher, even though she had already received an undergraduate degree in education.

We lived with my grandparents on my mother's side of the family for the first six months of my life. I've always been incredibly close to them, and from the beginning they always showed me love and compassion.

Grandma Betty babysat me everyday for two years. She took me everywhere and taught me a great deal about life, lessons that I have carried now for nineteen years.

When she went to the store, I tagged along with her. If we saw tractors on the way to the store, we'd stop and watch the workers. She imitated the tractor sounds, I imitated her imitation, and we laughed the whole time.

I loved our grocery store adventures because I had a major role in picking the vegetables that she cooked for supper. She'd set me in the grocery cart's seat and roam with me from aisle to aisle. We even made the tractor sounds in the cart sometimes, and caught a lot of attention from the other shoppers around us.

People often stared at me and I knew what they were curious about, even at such a young age. I finally asked her during one of our grocery store visits: "Grandma, why am I different from other kids?"

"God made you special, and it's okay to be different. No two people are ever going to be exactly the same," she answered. "Why would you wonder such a thing anyway?"

"I know when people are looking at me, because they look away when I look at them. I don't want people to feel afraid of me. I just want to be normal."

"You are perfectly normal. God loves you just as He loves everyone else in the store and all around the world. The next time you see someone who looks at you funny or someone you want to talk to, just say 'Hi, I'm Kyle,' and I promise you they won't ever be afraid to talk to you again."

Grandma Betty couldn't have been any wiser in how she taught me to treat people. I've learned that I should be the one to take the initiative and disarm people—no pun intended—if they have any fear about approaching me. I learned how to talk and interact with people by looking them in the eye, so they don't feel uncomfortable about glancing at my arms and legs.

As a child, I found someone in every aisle to say hello to, and with that pleasant greeting, most people were put at ease. It put me on a human level with them, where they could forget about feeling sorry for me for a moment—they could just view me as a young all-American boy.

The lesson of that experience has stuck with me for years. Whenever I greet an individual, I choose to shake their hand or give them a hug. I put out my arm for them to shake and say hello. Then they don't have the chance to feel uncomfortable around me.

I look everyone straight in the eye, as an equal, as God created all of us. Every one of us is a unique individual, and every one of us is equally precious in God's eyes. That's something I believe in my heart; it is part of my faith, and it is something my family taught me over and over again

There are so many small ways we can show this truth, just as my grandmother showed it to me through her actions. She decided that she wouldn't let an inaccessible playground stop her from taking me to play. When the mulch stopped my wheelchair's tires from going any further, she would carry me onto the slides, bars, and swing sets or into the forts. She was a playmate who refused to limit me to the confines of a wheelchair. As a child, it was just another innocent, normal part of life—playing in the park without a care in the world.

Grandma Betty used to let me use a paint brush and cover the walls with water. Once my Grandpa Norm even let me use real paint to help paint in their front entryway. He had just finished painting it himself, and I decided I wanted to help him, so he let me paint. He never did try to smooth it out. In fact, he would proudly point out my painting job to people.

My grandma loved taking me to restaurants because I loved to try everything. Egg rolls and mandarin noodles were my favorite foods at the age of two. When she cooked supper, I wanted to help. So she took a jellyroll pan and filled it with rice, beans, and cereal to show me how I could play construction with my toy tractors. Then again, my favorite part was when I would spill the pan on the carpet so I could use the vacuum cleaner and watch it all disappear.

Despite making messes, I eventually graduated to assistant chef. She set me down on the kitchen counter and I stirred, poured, turned the mixer on and off, or played with the sugar canister while she cooked. The sugar canister was a challenge with a sweet payoff. I worked and worked to get the scoop from inside the canister so I could get some sugar. Once in a while I did. Grandma was happy to see me working my arms, so it was okay with her if things got spilled. I was trying to help, and that was all that mattered.

Once I started to play outside more, my parents made a couple of special trips to the toy store to find things that I'd be able to play with outdoors. The other children had bicycles, but my favorite toy was an electric four-wheeler that my dad modified for me to drive. He took off the factory installed peddles and put a button on the handle bars so I could give it juice.

In the summertime, I'd drive it back and forth on our driveway, but if I didn't make the turns quick enough, I'd crash into the garage. The next step was to yell for one of my parents to come and turn me around so I could keep going. I wasn't strong enough to jump out and flip it around myself yet, and they got tired of helping me so often.

Eventually, my dad decided to rewire the yellow four-wheeler (that I called my Suzuki) and put a second button on the handle bars so that I could reverse it. I loved the fact that I could go anywhere with it and I was never jealous of the other kids in the neighborhood. They all played with their bikes, but hey—I had a hot rod!

While my dad always encouraged me to be more independent, he was also there whenever I needed help. No matter what it was, he was there with a solution. He'd cut the trigger guards off of squirt guns so I could play in the yard with my friends from the neighborhood. He even built me a bike, which he welded together himself, that I could peddle with my arms. There was never anything he couldn't fix or invent to make my childhood happier or more normal.

My childhood friends treated me in the simple, straightforward way that good kids do. They accepted me. We played capture the flag and cops and robbers. One of my parents or grandparents would pick me up and run me back and forth to follow the other kids. The older kids that were with us would help me too. And if there wasn't anyone there to carry me across the lawn, I'd start to bounce myself along. I was faster crawling on all fours, but I had to drop my squirt gun when

I did that, so the next best choice was to bounce back and forth. I was just as active as the other kids—I barely owned a pair of pants that didn't have grass stains all over them or holes from bouncing around in the street.

I remember feeling pretty exhausted at the end of the day, but I was having so much fun with my friends that I didn't want to quit playing. The other kids kept going—so why should I stop?

My favorite game was always street hockey. We could usually convince older kids to play street hockey against us, and even though the older players always pummeled us, we had a blast. In between our games, we'd wrestle around in the yard or find sharp stuff to make stick weapons out of—weapons that we never actually used, despite every mother's fears.

My dad bought me a regular hockey stick so I could play with the other kids, but he soon realized that my best position was goalie. He went out and bought a bigger goalie stick so I could block the shots, and he cut off the top of the stick so that I could hold it under my armpit to swivel it around.

I took competition seriously, even as a child. After I found a position that I could play well, I played street hockey every day with the kids in the neighborhood. The kids I played street hockey with didn't pick me to be goalie on their team because they felt sorry for me or wanted me to feel better by playing; it was because I worked hard and became skilled at the position. When teams were picked, I wasn't ever picked last or as a player a team got stuck with. The kids knew I wouldn't let anything pass me without a fight, and I got picked to play.

When I continued to improve, the kids tried to find different ways to score on me. At first they tried to go behind the net, but I was too quick to snatch the puck from them or block any shots that they took. There was almost no way that I'd let them score on me with a breakaway. They were all good, but there weren't any Wayne Gretzkys in the bunch to sneak around the net.

The only way that the kids found they were able to score easily on me was when they chipped the puck over my head. Everyone in the neighborhood agreed that it was a cheap way to score, so they lowered the top of the net to be level with my head. There was plenty of room left for them to take a shot and score, but they had to get past me first.

I took it as a compliment when other kids would try and chip the shot over my head, because that meant they were too afraid to take a shot straight at me. The lowered net was the only special privilege I received, and I still lost my share of games. My friends didn't take it easy on me when we played, or when we wrestled either—and that gave me all the more confidence that I could compete with everyone as an equal.

My first encounter with the media came as a direct result of the neighborhood street hockey games—a local newspaper reporter decided to do a feature story on us. My friends were excited, and we put together a four team tournament with three to four players on each team. I remember playing so much harder because I didn't want to disappoint the reporter if I let any goals slide past me.

The picture they chose to use for the article actually ended up foreshadowing my future passion for wrestling. Most of my friends and I were wrestling around in the yard and I didn't know they took that particular picture; it just happened to be the natural thing we did after our games.

Those same neighborhood friends gave me the first introduction I had to video games. I learned how to use a joystick and smash the right buttons, and eventually I could hold my own against the other kids. From the beginning, my favorite one was a pro-wrestling game on one of the older video gaming systems. Even to the older kids around us, I was still unbeatable at certain games on the Super Nintendo, and I used to compete with my dad nearly every night—he finally gave up trying to beat me.

When kids first played me in videogames, they sometimes thought they had to play easy on me—until I crushed them for the first time. I always thought the best part was when they tried their hardest, but I'd still beat them

I love new challenges and trying out new things. My parents thought I was crazy for spending all my allowance on video games, but I was on a mission to be the best that I could be at everything, to compete and win.

My Grandpa Norm and Grandma Betty gave me a little red and yellow car one Christmas that looked like a Volkswagen. At first, they pushed me around in the carpeted basement of their house. But they eventually got out of breath pushing me, and I wanted to go faster. So when the weather was nice, they pushed me around the neighborhood and to the park.

We'd stop to smell flowers on our walks, to let me sit in idle tractors, or to let me experiment trying to climb up trees. I was passionate about the Teenage Mutant Ninja Turtles at the time. They were costumed mutant heroes who supposedly lived in a sewer. There was a drainage sewer at the park, and my grandma and I would always stop at that spot so I could yell the character's names, "Raphael, Leonardo, Donatello, and Michelangelo!" down into the sewer.

I loved it when Grandpa came home from work. I've always had a special relationship with him. One of my favorite things to do was to use the jump rope and "tie" Grandpa up as he lay on the floor. I would spend an hour doing that, moving deliberately, wrapping the rope around and around his legs. We'd wrestle around on the ground, and he said that what I didn't know was that he was getting to rest while I tied him up.

I developed competitive tenacity at a very young age. I did not like to give up on anything.

My grandpa and I played a lot of baseball in the basement. I had a big red bat and he would throw a plastic softball or tennis ball for me to hit. I never had any trouble hitting the ball, and we even laid down bases that I ran or bounced around.

My body's coordination got sharper over time, and I got stronger. After I got a little older, but still not very big, I became too strong for playing ball in the basement. The tennis balls went flying towards windows and lamps, so we had to take the game outside from then on.

During the Christmas season when I was three years old, my Grandma and Grandpa took me to eat a quick supper at a nearby restaurant, and then to see the Christmas lights downtown. We passed a downtown fire station where the firefighters had just returned from a blaze. We knocked on the door, and they let us into the firehouse and showed us their station and the fire truck. I got to sit in the driver's seat and pretend like I was driving it.

They asked if I'd like them to turn on the siren, but my grandparents thought that would be too much for a three year old. So instead, they staged a mock fire alert for us. The firefighters were notified of the mock fire, and then they all came sliding down the pole, ready to jump in the truck. I remember marveling at the heroism of these men in their gear, always ready to ride out and help people in need.

Church has always played an important role in my family, and we always went to church on Sundays. Until I was nearly seven, Grandpa Norm went with me to my Sunday School classes while my parents were in theirs. If I needed to use scissors in Sunday School, he'd do the cutting and I would do the coloring and pasting. I loved watching the music minister in church, and I started directing the musicians, trying to imitate him. The pastor at our church told me that I could be a director of music some day.

At this time, doctors were trying to fit me with prostheses for my arms and legs. I found that to be a difficult adjustment. Sometimes I would wear the artificial legs to church, and if we played "Duck, Duck, Goose," my Grandpa would pick me up and run around the circle, chasing after whoever tagged me.

My Grandpa retired by the time I was in fourth grade, and he was able to be my helper on field trips too. The field trips gave me the opportunity to go right along with my classmates, doing and experiencing everything they did. It also gave me a lot of valuable time bonding with my Grandpa.

My Physical Education class went to a local YMCA for swim sessions. The sessions extended over several weeks, and we always had one session per week. There was a special lady instructor assigned to help me, and she worked with my Grandpa to help me in the water.

At first I felt very apprehensive about being in deep water, since all the water in the pool was over my head. But the longer we swam, the more comfortable I felt. It was just another challenge that I overcame. Now that I'm older, I'm able to swim for long distances, and water is a friend.

There are so many things from my childhood that stand out in retrospect as having a real impact on my life. I remember the days with my parents and grandparents so vividly—the trips to the park, wrestling with neighborhood kids, learning to be more independent and starting to value competition.

Most of all, I remember the cave.

When I was in fourth grade, I joined the Cub Scouts and my dad was a leader of the pack. The longest field trip that we took was to a cave in Southern Indiana. My Cub Scout Pack spent a night in the cave, along with several other Scout groups.

It was March and cold outside, but the temperature inside the cave was a constant 58 degrees all year long. It was dark and dank.

There was a stream running through the cave. The stream was narrow inside, but it exited the cave as a river. We took a boat ride down the stream in the cave, and we saw bats and other cave creatures.

We spread plastic sheets over the freezing ground and spent the night in sleeping bags near the stream. No one slept very much that night. The cold from the ground soon seeped through the plastic sheets and into the sleeping bags. We all felt cold and a little spooked by the dark.

The highlight of the night, before we went to bed, was a trip through the deeper section of the cave. We adventured single file through a portion of the cave, the local guides in front and back of us. As always, I wanted to be in the front, right behind the leader.

We had to crawl through a narrow two hundred foot corridor. The rock above our heads was so low that we had to slither on our stomachs like snakes. There were a couple of inches of water below us. There was no avoiding getting wet, because the rock ceiling was so low. Everyone had hard hats and flashlights, and my dad attached a miner's light to my hard hat.

It seemed like it was hard work for everyone else, including my Grandfather (who was along as a chaperone), but I excelled, and wanted to push the pace. It was a perfect environment for me. I'd always crawled on all fours and loved the dirt and mud inside the cave. I felt the exhilaration of discovery, and I wanted to go farther and deeper than anyone else.

What I realized at that point was that everyone has certain abilities that they can learn to use, no matter who they are. The conditions inside of the cave were ideal for me, and I could've carried on for miles if I needed to, while the other people with us were exhausted after we'd gone sixty yards. The cave environment was tailored for my body, just as I would soon find to be true in the case of certain football positions or wrestling moves.

I will return to the cave someday and explore on my own. The cave taught me that I could be the best at whatever I wanted to do if I found the right way to do it.

I know there are many people who, whether they admit it or not, view disabled people as inferior. We are "broken" in their eyes - we are of no use, no value, and we are just running out the string on life. But I believe that we are all disabled in one way or another - including disabilities of character and personality. My disability just happens to be more visual than some.

CHAPTER 4 Growing Up Normal

My sister and closest friend, Amber-Leigh Maynard, was born April 30, 1988. I remember holding her in the hospital when she was born, the feel of her cradled close to me. For as long as I can remember, I promised myself that I would do anything it took to teach, protect, and love her as a brother.

The waiting room in the hospital was dimly lit, but her brightness changed all that as she came into the world. When my parents let me hold her on my own, I felt responsible, and filled with a distinct kind of love that can only be shared between siblings.

My parents and family had understandable concerns that Amber would suffer birth defects similar to my own. But genetic research assured my parents they had no reason to worry. My condition has unknown causes, but it is not a congenital defect that is carried on.

Amber quickly became my friend and playmate in the house, and we used to run all over the place with toy guns and action figures. We'd run up and down the stairs, run inside, run outside. We were just as active and rowdy as a normal brother and sister.

My sister never made a fuss about our physical differences. Ironically, this was partly because I wasn't burdened by the prosthetic limbs and devices that completely stripped me of my ability to move.

On my first day of kindergarten, my physical therapist recommended that I wear the prosthetic arms and legs that were fitted for me. They were supposed to be for functional and aesthetic purposes, but they didn't look natural at all when they were bound to my body with intricate straps. I hated them.

I couldn't move without someone constantly helping me with the artificial limbs. If I was seated, then I couldn't stand on my own. If I was standing, then someone had to help me land in a seat. The prosthetic limbs became a heavy burden for me and those around me.

The legs connected to my hips and had cups that were specially designed for me to fit my feet into. Sweat had to be poured out of them just so I could stay in the legs for more than an hour at a time.

The arms weren't any better. There was a jumbled mess of straps that connected all across my shoulders and back. In order to open the crab-like hands, I had to move my back and shoulders in such a way to tug the straps and open or release the grip.

When I decided to take one of my toy guns to the kindergarten class for show and tell, my mother watched me from behind a window. I had no idea she was there, but she watched as the teacher carried me from my seat to the center of the circle with my prosthetic arms and legs on. I sat there, unable to do or show anything to my friends in the class.

I fumbled quietly with the plastic gun until my time was up and I had to be carried to my seat once again. My mom watched as the class worked on their coloring exercises and I could barely keep up, the awkward prosthetic arms slowing me down.

When the teacher explained to the class that I would be coming to school without my prosthetics from then on, the children happily approved. The freedom of being rid of those things was exhilarating. I knew then that I wanted to live my life as much as possible without false prosthetic restraints.

My next two beautiful sisters, Lindsay and MacKenzie, added to our loving family. Lindsay was born six years after me, and MacKenzie is nine years younger than me. The four of us grew up supporting each other and competing in everything.

Lindsay showed a ridiculous amount of coordination even when she was a toddler, and it wasn't long before she was roughhousing with Amber and me. By the time MacKenzie was born, I was desperate for a brother to grow up with. I was close with the girls, and we played together all the time, but I wanted a brother who would be as much of a sports fan as I was.

My parents made two decisions after MacKenzie was born: I was going to be stuck without a brother, so I had better get used to it—and we were going to move from our home in Fort Wayne, Indiana and head to Suwanee, Georgia, a suburb of Atlanta.

My sisters and I felt like our world had been crushed when we heard the news that we were moving. It made sense for the family, of course—my grandparents were heading to Georgia, so my family decided to pack up and go too. But this was the only place we had ever known. My friends, crushes, teachers, and the comforts of familiarity were stripped away.

Amber and I went ballistic as the movers came in and broke down the furniture in our home to move it all away. We screamed, cried, and said horrible things to our parents, even though they only wanted the best for us. My mother assured us that we'd find new friends and have a better life in Georgia, but I resented the fact that our parents were forcing us to move with all of my heart. I never wanted to find new friends; I had plenty in Indiana.

The fact was, for all my competitiveness, I had a deep-seated insecurity that I had never made the effort to change. I had no confidence in my ability to branch out and meet new people; I was afraid that new people would never see me as just Kyle—they would see me as the kid born without arms and legs. It was the first time I truly felt afraid. But I had more advantages to build on than I knew.

My mother had always made it a point to make sure that I was a well-dressed, well-groomed, and well-mannered child. Because of her help, I knew how to make friends and have an active social life. I certainly felt I was an accepted and popular kid in Indiana. In fact, I had all the cool friends; and I knew one of reasons no one would ever say anything to make fun of me was because I had those friends, because I wasn't a loner, because I was popular and didn't have to prove myself to everyone.

In elementary school in Indiana, I had a huge crush on a beautiful young blonde-haired girl named Whitney, who I've been lucky enough to stay in touch with after all these years. At the time, I couldn't bring myself to approach her and let her know how I felt because I was afraid of her reaction to me. I was afraid my disability would get in the way of talking to her.

Other kids in the fourth grade had their first romances, and I grew to be envious of the fact that they were normal and I was obviously not. I thought she'd reject me because I was in a wheelchair.

I had no self-confidence when it came to girls. That was one time when I compared myself to others and found myself lacking. I thought there was no way she could love me.

Moving to Georgia, I initially felt as intimidated as I did with the blonde-haired girl in Indiana. I was scared to ride my wheelchair inside the school. I was afraid kids would laugh or make fun of me.

Fifth grade can be a rough time in any child's life. But that's especially true when you have to start over and make an entirely new set of friends in a new school in a new neighborhood. It's even worse when you have the knowledge going in that you're not like other kids. Not only was I afraid for myself, but I was also afraid I'd disappoint my family if I wasn't able to pull it off, make new friends, and settle in.

What I didn't count on was my mother and my family who, of course, all treated me the same as before. I wasn't moving alone; I was moving with those who loved me most.

It was at that point—when I finally understood that my greatest support was my family—that I realized what I needed to do wasn't worry or complain about the move, but build my self-confidence. I realized that before people would ever accept me, I had to accept myself and the fact that I was different. I made the conscious decision to accept myself and my difference, and move forward.

I determined that I could make any friend I wanted to—I just had to make other people feel comfortable around me; if I did that, they could accept me without fear.

My social life blossomed shortly after we moved to Georgia. People gravitate to others who have confidence. Within days after Amber and I enrolled in the school, I knew that we had the confidence we needed to make new friends. In fact, when I realized what a fool I had been about moving, I was much more concerned with Amber's well-being than my own. I wanted her to be happy and cultivate the same kind of friendships I was quickly developing.

Sure, I could still see doubt in people's eyes when they first met me, but I made it a goal to dispel that doubt, to make them realize that I was just another human being, just another schoolboy.

One of my best friends was a young kid from New York named Joey Leonardo—as soon as we met, we realized that we both had a whole lot in common with one another. We spent almost every night and day hanging out, playing video games and just being kids down at the neighborhood pool.

The reason why Joey is so unique from any other friend that I've made before was the fact that he has never looked at me like I had a disability at all. We've faced a number of challenges together, but that has only brought us closer. To this day, each of us has a second home in one another's house. Our friendship began by having so many common interests, but has grown into a brotherhood that both of us would fight to protect.

Joey's brother, Chris, is only two years younger than us. By growing up with the Leonardo brothers, I was able to feel that I had brothers of my own. We motivate each other to be better people, competitors, and friends. They know they can push me harder than almost anyone else, and they understand how I live my life.

If we're playing Halo 2 on Xbox and I'm not playing to my fullest potential, they will get on my case about it. I never turn and make excuses by saying something ridiculous but true in response, such as: "I don't have hands to hit all the buttons, so lay off." They know that because I don't make excuses, the only reaction that will come out of saying something along those lines is an improvement in my focus and playing ability.

Even in this trivial circumstance, excuses are simply the way to avoid an obstacle without giving any effort to conquer it. Excuses give us a reason to explain to other people why we are too weak to deal with a particular problem, regardless of the size or importance of the matter.

PRAISE FOR BROKEN PEOPLE

I know that God made me the way that I am for a reason. Maybe the reason is to make other people comfortable with themselves and their own God-given abilities. I'm still finding that out—and I know that process starts with facing these issues head on.

There are many people who, whether they admit it or not, view disabled people as inferior. We are "broken" in their eyes—we're of no use, no value, and we're just running out the string on life.

Perhaps these people think we should never have been born, that our parents would have been more responsible to abort us, because our quality of life isn't as high as society thinks it should be in order to be valuable. Needless to say, my parents and I disagree. I love my life; I know the great power of life and love. And I think that those who consider disabled people "broken" fail to see that while some of us have disabilities that are physically obvious, in truth all people are disabled in one way or another—including disabilities of character and personality.

A friend referred me to a quote from Whittaker Chambers in his book *Witness*, where he wrote to his children: "For when you understand what you see, you will no longer be children. You will know that life is pain, that each of us hangs always upon the cross of himself. And when you know that this is true of every man, woman, and child on earth, you will be wise."

We all, in that sense, have our cross to bear.

My parents did not know that I would be born with a disability. But disabilities that we can see *in utero* have caused complications for parents who see their child on the sonogram screen. Naturally, parents have distinct fears regarding their child's future if there is a potentially life-altering abnormality.

When my mother was pregnant for the first time, the technology wasn't as sophisticated as it is now, when obstetricians can get a better picture of any deformities a baby may have. Had the technology been capable and my parents willing to go that route, I wouldn't be here today. But my mother has told me many times that even if she had known, she wouldn't have aborted me.

Many parents have difficulty dealing with the fear of the unknown, fear of what a disabled child will face. At this point, parents hold the balance of life and death—and almost always, the choice that seems easiest, that seems the most convenient, is death. In the end, many choose to abort, giving up on their child before he or she has the chance to live.

I don't know how many cases like mine have happened, but I know that many parents might not have had the courage to face the challenge the way my parents did. I don't know how many other Kyle Maynards may have been out there—we never will.

About a year ago, radio shock jock Howard Stern asked me to appear on his morning show. He had seen a special about my life and wanted to ask me some questions. Many of my friends thought it could be a mistake to go on his show because of his reputation for saying and doing controversial things, but I accepted. The show went off without a hitch. More than that, in the course of the interview, Howard said that having met me now, he would definitely reconsider aborting a baby with missing limbs.

I know that doctors sometimes advise abortion, but I also know that doctors aren't always right. Most doctors also try to promote the use of prosthetics early on instead of allowing for other options down the road.

I've heard numerous stories about doctors who operate on children to make it easier to fit the prostheses on limbs. These surgeries can help sometimes, but usually end up having very negative consequences in the end. When I was an infant some doctors suggested I have similar surgeries done. I'm fortunate that my parents got multiple opinions before putting me under the chopping block.

I'm not a surgeon or a doctor, of course, but I do know I wouldn't be here today if my parents hadn't chosen life, and I wouldn't be able to do many of the day-to-day activities if I didn't have use of my feet, which might have been removed in a surgical procedure for prosthetics I don't need. When I meet parents with disabled children, I encourage them to wait, if possible, before any major surgeries are done, because it's likely their child will grow to adapt to what he or she has been given.

There's no reason to make life more difficult by burdening a child with surgeries or heavy prosthetics that he or she really doesn't need, especially if the only goal is to use prosthetics to make a child look normal. It's not easy to be a parent of a disabled child who isn't old enough to help make these decisions, but it's a part of the responsibility that comes with any child. There are more important things than giving a false impression of normalcy. What's really normal is to be yourself, and to do as much as you can do.

I'm happy to say that shortly after my family moved to Georgia, everyone I encountered on a daily basis began to see me the same way that I saw myself. The differences were less important than what we had in common. They didn't see me as broken. They saw me as normal. Without the wheelchair, I was the same kid at heart that they were.

We all have to do our part to banish the entrenched negative way of thinking and fight the belief that the disabled are broken people. We need to enable one another by showing through our actions that we value all life, whether society views a person as normal or not, and by being a support for each other in real and emotional ways.

As human beings, our inability to be the very best at everything means we must rely on other people to help us where we are lacking. We have to embrace that common bond—it's the true nature of living a full life with our fellow man.

It's natural for people to doubt me because of my appearance, but the limits others place on me often become a burden. Even as a child, I understood the importance of credibility. So I make it a point to always show who I am by actions and not simply by words, to back things up instead of making false promises. That way people can take heart and believe in me.

CHAPTER 5 **Trying Out to Wear #8**

or a number of weeks, I listened to my new fifth grade friends in Georgia talk about the sports they played and how much fun they were having. I was a sports fanatic just like they were.

We loved the Atlanta Braves, Hawks, and Falcons. The local professionals were our heroes, and I couldn't survive the day without watching ESPN. At school we'd talk about what had happened to our favorite players and teams the night before. All of our conversations were centered on sports, and we were obsessed as only ten-year-old boys can be.

The only times I dropped out of our discussions was when my friends told stories about their football, basketball, or baseball games from the previous day. I was glad they did so well in their respective sports, but I ached to play in an organized league just like they did.

Whenever they talked about their games at the lunch table, I would imagine myself playing alongside them on their teams. I imagined myself being the savior of the championship game by catching the football for a touchdown or scoring the last second winning basket.

At home I dreamt about being a professional athlete and playing on one of my favorite Atlanta sports teams. My dreams made me the star athlete who performed coolly under pressure; I'd imagine replacing John Smoltz as the clutch pitcher on the mound for the Atlanta Braves in the middle of their pennant race.

In my dreams, the only limitation was my imagination—the real world was different. I never thought the dream world, where I was the star, would be any different from the real world. In my mind's eye, the only difference was that now I'd be playing for real.

The more stories I heard about how much fun my friends were having, the more I wanted to play alongside them. My passion for sports and my drive to succeed were enough, I told myself—I would stop at nothing in my pursuit to be a normal fifth grade student and a great competitor.

More than anything else, I wanted to be the quarterback who dated the cutest cheerleader and became an icon among my peers. I was convinced that football was my avenue to reach out for those dreams.

My parents often had different emotions about my ambition to try new things. My father would dream alongside of me; my mother kept my feet on the ground. She told me to focus on the things I could do; my dad, like me, thought I could do more if I just worked hard enough.

My mom is as close to my heart as anyone else, but her fear of my disappointment has always clashed with my stubborn belief that I can do anything. No one wants to see their child's passions lead to emotional letdown. She tried to teach me to see the success in whatever I did, even when I failed. She is a great supporter, and I've always valued her advice, even when my enthusiasm for things like football meant that I didn't always follow it.

I couldn't have been more excited when I brought home a flyer from school about the upcoming football tryouts. The teacher who passed me the flyer—after I asked her for one—was surprised to see me so animated about it. She obviously didn't see me as a football player.

My mother couldn't help but feel a twinge of sadness when she saw the joy in my face, because she knew the likelihood of my making the team wasn't great. My dad was out of town at the time and he wasn't there to fan my dream. So my mother and I had a long conversation about my expectations and the possibility of failure.

She made it clear to me that the odds were I'd end up as a water boy for the team, on the sideline instead of the field. But she thought I'd have fun, make a lot of friends by being a part of the team, and make my own contribution to it. I agreed with everything she said, silently knowing that I ultimately wanted to be an important athlete on the team.

My mom is much more social and outgoing than I am or my father is. Rather than just show up, she called the coach to ask him if I could tryout. She made it clear that I was very different from other kids he had coached, but she never implied that I couldn't be a player. Neither my father nor I would have had the guts to call the coach in the first place, but my mother did it out of her love for me. And while telling the coach I was different, she never said I couldn't do what would be asked of me.

The next day, she took me to the tryouts. Football wasn't her favorite sport, but it didn't matter. Even then, I appreciated that very few mothers would have taken a disabled son to tryout for a football team full of able-bodied kids; she did it out of love for me, and I loved her for it.

We drove into the community's park for the first time and saw all of the football and baseball fields. The park was full of kids using the batting cages and basketball courts. My mom pushed me along in my wheelchair. When we got close to the field, I jumped out and ran to where the kids were gathered to try out for the football team. I was relieved to see a lot of my friends from school were at the tryouts to. I asked some of my friends about what I should expect. They told me about the drills, and I saw no reason why I couldn't excel at them. I was a kid, I was finally at the football tryouts, and it was time for me to do my thing.

The first drill was a timed forty yard dash down the field. I was a little nervous as the line kept moving and it was closer to my turn. When it was my turn at last, I stepped up to the starting line. The assistant coach asked me if I'd be able to do the drill, and I gave him a nod of confidence. When he gave me the signal to go, I sprinted off as hard as I could.

I was in a dead sprint in my bear-crawl stance, which means all four of my limbs were on the ground and I ran like an animal. Then suddenly, halfway through the first forty yard dash, I ran into a big problem. The baggy t-shirt I was wearing slipped up my back and started to come off fast once I picked up speed. My arms were tripped up—so I immediately bucked myself up on my back legs and waved my arms to pull the shirt down.

As fast as I shot up to fix the problem, I was back down to the sprint. Everyone watching was impressed at the fact that I had run so fast, and there was a lot of applause coming from the parents on the sideline. The head coach came up to me after the drill was finished and told me he was very eager to have me play on his team.

I was incredibly thrilled to have done so well and shown everyone, myself included, that I could be a part of an organized and talented football team. We finished the tryouts with a couple of drills to test our agility, and I performed well. Then the coach directed prospective players about how to register for the team.

At the registration I had the opportunity to have a closer conversation with the coach, whose name was Tom Schie. He told me that I was picked for his team because of the ability I showed to play the game, and not for any other reason than that. Coach Schie also told me that he had a good idea of what position I'd be playing, but that I had to wait until the first day of practice to find out what it was.

Of course, I really assumed that I'd be the quarterback, and I chose number eight for my jersey because it was the same number of one of my sports heroes, Troy Aikman. I always loved Aikman's toughness under pressure and ability to play through pain. Electrified for the season to start, I went home after the registration and patiently waited for the first practice.

I went to the store with my father, and we bought additional padding to help protect my arms and legs. Since I wasn't able to wear shoes and I walked around on my arms, it was very important to have some type of protective covering on my limbs.

My dad decided to sew the ends of arm pads together to protect the ends of my arms and legs. After I got my shoulder pads and helmet, I couldn't help but stare at the equipment pile for weeks, dreaming about the upcoming season.

The tryouts were in the beginning of the summer after fifth grade, but the season didn't actually start until after school began again in the fall. For once in my life, I couldn't wait for school to start.

TRAINING FOR STRENGTH

As the summer started to wind down, my dad and I attended the unofficial weight training to get ready for the first practice. We got some weight training equipment that would work for me, so that I could lift with the team and get in shape. I needed some type of strap to fit around the ends of my arms and some way to attach weight to those straps in order for me to pull it with resistance.

We happened to find a remarkable piece of equipment that was able to do exactly what we were looking for. We took leather straps from ankle bands that were designed for leg extensions with high weight resistance. The straps came with rope to attach them to machines, and we looped the rope through free-weights. I would lift the free-weights and get a workout with a full range of motion.

My father helped me through my first experience lifting in the high school weight room. A few of the high school football players were lifting when my sixth grade friends and I started our workouts. I remember seeing one of the high school linebackers lift up and shrug an obscene amount of weight over and over again. He was a gigantic man in comparison to my sixty pound frame.

My father was there to help me and show me the correct way to weight train, but all I could focus on was the intensity in the faces of the high school varsity players who were working out. I never thought that I'd be able to get that intense without someone screaming in my face after every repetition.

My dad forced me to start out lifting with very light weight at the start of the weight training and conditioning practices. He told me it was very important to establish my form with each lift before I tried to increase the weight.

He made me start out with an embarrassingly weak two and a half pounds for each arm. The total of five pounds was easy to lift, but I did learn a great deal about form and technique. My dad gave me instructions for every exercise I was capable of doing with the weights. The first exercise I did was a butterfly press (a modified bench press), laying down on my back and facing up towards the ceiling. The next was a curl type motion from the same position, with my back on the topside of the bench. Then he had me try a set of pull downs.

Those three exercises were crucial in developing my shoulder strength and are solely responsible, in my opinion, for why I haven't suffered a serious shoulder injury in the course of my wrestling and weightlifting career. As my strength grew, I was able to perform the exercises faster and with greater weights.

The next series of exercises started from a seated position on the floor. For the crucifix exercise, I extended my arms with weights attached straight out to my sides and moved them up and down for a repetition. Those were followed by front lateral raises with the weights directly in front of me. I lifted them from the floor, working the front of my shoulders. The last exercise my father taught me came from the face-down position on the bench press, and I pulled the weights up off of the floor and into a rowing motion to strengthen my back muscles.

I combined those exercises with a few of my own, such as my pushups, which for me are really a variation of a handstand. I did a great deal of those to strengthen my chest and shoulders. Sit-ups and weightless squats were the only other exercises that I initially trained with—in time, I'd come to learn more about what my body was capable of doing.

But, regardless of how much I learned about weight training during the first session, I was still incredibly embarrassed by the fact that the varsity high school players saw me lifting with two and a half pounds tied to ropes on each arm.

Now as an experienced lifter, there was never any reason for me to feel embarrassed at all. The high school kids were probably excited to see me try if anything at all. And even if they didn't know it at the time, they helped to motivate my strength and passion for lifting. After watching them throw huge amounts of weight around with ease, I told myself that I'd be able to do the same thing one day.

The weight training prepared me to step onto the practice field for the first day of conditioning work. We had to show up wearing just our helmets. The coaches wanted us to get used to wearing them while we worked hard. We ran sprints up and down the field to warm up.

I was incredibly exhausted by the end of the exercise, more so than my teammates. While they were running normal sprints, I had to run on all fours with much shorter and faster steps in each stride.

It was excruciating working to keep up with the rest of the team, but I had to. I had to prove to the coaches that I could play. I couldn't provide them a reason to give up on me.

When we finished the night's conditioning, I walked over to my dad at the side of the field. He helped me unsnap the chinstrap on my helmet, and I felt the collection of steam and sweat lift off my head as the helmet came off for the first time.

After the practice, my muscles tensed up and got sore real fast. My neck ached all night long from lifting the helmet up the entire practice. I had never experienced such an intense workout as I did with that first football practice.

We had the same conditioning style practice the next day, and it continued for the duration of the week. I couldn't have been happier when the conditioning practices finally ended, but they got easier each time because now I knew what to do. I felt stronger as the days passed.

Now that the conditioning practices were finished, we were at last able to put on our shoulder pads and prepare for a battle in the trenches. I was taught that I should practice as I would play, and that meant going all out on every single drill that we did.

I found out from the coaches that my position would be the team's nose tackle. The nose tackle is a defensive lineman whose purpose is to cause havoc on the line of scrimmage. My goal was to do everything I could to mess up the offense's play, and never let the football cross a three foot gap that I protected as if my life depended upon it.

We stretched out at the beginning of practice, and after that, the first drill was called "Oklahoma," an exercise to work on our blocking and tackling ability. Two linemen from the offense would line up against two linemen from the defense, and a ball carrier had to cross a three foot gap in between two heavy bags that were laid out as boundaries.

My job, as a defensive lineman, was to stop the ball carrier from passing me at all costs. My personal objective was to ram my body into the legs of the ball carrier and knock him to the ground. I wanted to plant my face mask in the ball carrier's thigh and drill his legs with enough force to make it impossible for him to keep moving.

Good carriers met the tackle with a force of their own and with the loud smack—and pain—that came with each rock-solid collision. But the competitive fires were burning within me, and I became addicted to dishing out pain of my own to anyone who stood in my way.

The team came together for a competitive scrimmage after the drills were finished. Our offensive starters squared off against the defense, and it was the first time I had a chance to showcase my true abilities as a football player.

Everything we had done up until this point—the tryouts, weight-lifting, conditioning practices, and technique drills—all had a purpose, but couldn't be an accurate representation of a player's full ability. The only time you can get a really good feel for judging the ability of a prospective player is to see what the athlete has to offer when it counts.

Even though we were only scrimmaging, it counted just as much as a game to the players and the coaches who were watching. The coaches had decisions to make about which players would get the most playing time, and each of the players desperately wanted to play as much as possible.

I knew that I—more than any of the others—needed to show the coaches my ability to play in a real situation and perform as well as I did in practice.

I lined up directly across from a friend of mine at school. He was the center offensive lineman and the kid responsible for snapping the ball back to the quarterback. When he walked to the line and put his hand on the ball, my mind went into tunnel vision.

I watched his fingers grip the football's laces as he took his three-point stance. He squatted down with the other linemen. I could tell he saw the look of determination in my eyes. I saw his hands tense, and seconds later his arm shot back to bring the ball into the quarterback's hands. My heart raced with anticipation when I saw the ball move right in front of me for the very first time.

Purely out of instinct, I shot my body under his legs before he could react and figure out how to block me. I pushed my body through so fast that I was disoriented when I passed the center, but I could see the ball and knew that I needed to attack in that direction.

The center was so confused that I had passed under his legs that he gave up on trying to block me. I tackled the ball carrier before he could make a move.

The rest of the practice was an incredible tug of war. Because the center knew not to let me under his legs, he dropped his body down to my level after the ball was snapped. That turned into a constant battle between the two of us.

I knew from Coach Schie's instructions that defensive linemen have to keep fighting to make the tackle. If the offensive linemen tried to block me in one direction, I knew he was trying to move me away from the ball. But I still had a few surprises left after the dive through my competitor's legs.

One of the things I worked on with my father was a move that we called the "butt roll"—it was a simple spin to clear off the pressure from the offensive linemen. I only weighed about 65 pounds, and some offensive linemen were more than double my weight. But the butt roll freed me to get around them and get to the ball carrier.

The butt roll became my patented move, and there were very few times that another kid could keep me from getting to where I wanted to be, regardless of his size advantage. I hit that roll over and over again before the opposing team's lineman could ever figure out where I was headed. By spinning my body around with the butt roll, I was able to cross over the line of scrimmage and get behind the offensive linemen. That way, they couldn't knock me off the line, and I could disrupt the action in their backfield.

The other advantage I had was to keep the offensive lineman constantly guessing which way I would be heading. If he anticipated my spin move, then he would be off-balance if I plowed into him like a bull and knocked him back off the line of scrimmage.

When I got myself into a position against the ball carrier, I would dig in and nothing could get me out. Once I was where I needed to be on the line of scrimmage, it was all over; I wouldn't let running backs through my domain.

Another advantage I had over the opposing team was that I was so low to the ground. No opposing players could get lower than me, and that was a huge advantage because I was so difficult to move. They had to resort to using their weight and momentum to slam me back before I established my position.

Being so low to the ground also meant that the ball carriers on opposing teams couldn't concentrate on looking to see if they were going to be stopped by me or stopped by the linebackers behind me. When the ball carriers on the offense were looking to see whether or not they could run past the linebackers, I was able to make a move to take out their legs. And even if the running back from the opposing team was looking for me near the ground, then he couldn't possibly focus on the linebackers behind me, making for an easy tackle.

PART OF THE TEAM

Football taught me what team building was all about. I had to trust my teammates to make the tackles, and they in turn had to trust in my ability to do the same. Trust is incredibly important when you're suddenly met with a challenge that will not only call upon your best efforts, but will also demand the same ethic from everyone around you.

There were ten other players on the field on my team. We each had an equally important job. I expected them to do theirs with everything they had, and they expected the same of me. If I couldn't do it—well, I had no business being on the field.

Through my actions, I showed that I wasn't disabled on the football field. I was a member of a team that had an objective. We had to shut the other team's offense down or we would fail.

The only way I could prove myself worthy of starting on the team was if I gave my fullest effort every single play and accepted the fact that I may have to play harder than the average player.

The coaches noticed my ability, determination, and the progress I made in practice, but for our first game, they decided not to start me. I waited on the bench for my chance to get in the game. I had given so much effort to try to break the starting lineup that I couldn't help but feel discouraged. But I knew I hadn't worked hard enough, that I had to push myself in practice harder than I had before to make sure I was heard. I had to push myself harder than I thought physically possible. That's what I had to do if I wanted to make the starting squad.

I regrouped, focused mentally, and worked unbelievably hard for the next few weeks. I knew that the harder I worked, the more playing time Coach Schie and the other coaches would decide to give me.

Everyone understood how difficult it was for me to do everything that was required to start on the team. I had to deliver an out of mind performance and never make a noticeable mistake. The second I made a mistake, the coaches would notice and doubt my playing ability; so I pressured myself to never let them have that doubt. I left myself no margin for error. I would not let people see me fail.

The head coach, Tom Schie, was the only man, aside from my father, who thought I had a legitimate chance to play if I continued to work hard. Without Coach Schie's help and encouragement, I might never have become an athlete in any sport. I worked to prove to the coaches that if I played, my total focus would be on my job and helping our team win. I wouldn't let them down. In practice, I did anything and everything to make sure that I was prepared to play when my time came.

I didn't make any excuses for why the coaches decided not to start me. I didn't quit or give up. I met the adversity with a full head of steam. When the emotion and tenacity boiled over the top, I became an animal. I was as possessed as a pit-bull in pursuit of the ball carrier. It didn't matter who was lined up across from me. I wanted to make them feel pain, because I wanted to change the way players and coaches saw me; not as a disabled player, but as a defensive lineman who could inflict more damage than anyone else had before.

Each time my face mask smashed against the opposing player's legs I could feel my neck rattle under the pressure. It was quite possible that it could've been broken in a single hit, but just like my fervor for football, it held strong. I was rattled and beaten down that I wasn't the starter for the team, but I was learning one of the most valuable lessons that life could ever teach me.

We are all knocked down in the dirt at some point in our lives. But only the strong will rise again, brush themselves off, and move on to conquer and win. That strength comes from inside you, from your family and your faith.

I had a lot of support from my family. Their encouragement kept me pushing hard. And prayer and faith kept me going whenever I felt uncertain.

I loved playing the game of football. I loved hitting and tackling as a nose tackle. But I had a hard time accepting the fact that I would never reach the levels of performance I wanted, and never achieve my dream of being a star quarterback.

I prayed that God would help show me what I needed to do—and I believe He did. Through prayer, I accepted the fact that we aren't all meant to be stars on the team, but that we each have a purpose. To find that purpose, we need to live the life that God has planned for us. I realized that I needed to make the decisions that God wanted me to make, not necessarily those I wanted to make. So I kept working hard, but I left the ultimate outcome of all my efforts in God's hands.

Initially, the coaches only gave me the opportunity to play when the team was winning by a lot and they could afford some mistakes.

They didn't have full faith in my potential to do well when the game was on the line. But I was committed to proving them wrong.

When I had a chance to play, I made the most of it by doing everything I could to shut down the offense on the line of scrimmage. More times than not, I'd be able to play for four to five plays at a time. That usually gave the coaches on the opposing team the chance to run the ball at me to see if they could score a few easy yards.

I was relentless in my attack on our game days. The opposing coach would soon refuse to run the ball anywhere near me when he saw how intense I laid my helmet into his running back. There was no man that could pass me when I was focused and prepared to do damage and earn my position on the starting team.

Coach Schie saw my desire. He knew I wouldn't let him down by not giving my fullest effort every single play that I was in the game. As a consequence, he started giving me a lot more playing time.

He would put me in as a fresh lineman when the score was close or even if we were down by a few points. As his confidence grew in me, my confidence grew in myself. And that confidence helped make me a better and more versatile athlete because I could play with more intensity. I loved playing the game, I loved helping the team, and I loved having the chance to prove myself on every down.

There was one instance where a coach from an opposing team told my coach he was going to "take it easy on the little guy in the middle." Coach Schie went berserk and made it very clear that I was an athlete there to compete, not a mascot for the team or someone who wanted people to feel sorry for him.

Coach Schie used his conversation with the other team's coach as our pre-game pep talk. My friends and teammates all went nuts. I became a motivator for them, not just a token member of the football team.

Coach Schie gave me a lot of playing time in that game, and the opposing coach ran the ball right at me the very first play that I came in. He did it with his largest running back, purposefully to spite my coach.

I was determined not to allow him to embarrass my team or my coach. I crushed the running back with all of the strength that I had in me. He went stumbling back, and my teammates joined me to make the gang tackle.

The coach didn't run a single play in my direction for the remainder of the game.

I live to be tested under stressful situations and to pull through in the clutch, but this time I was also defending the respect of my coach and my teammates, and it was a great feeling to succeed.

On the football field, I never made excuses. I wanted to succeed for my father, to make him proud of my ability to play the game. I wanted to make tackles for all my friends and teammates who knew I would never let them down. I wanted to make plays for Coach Schie, who truly believed in my dedication and abilities. And I wanted to reward my mother's dedication to me—thanks to her realism, I felt even better when good things happened.

My first girlfriend, in the sixth grade, was another tremendous motivator for me. She was always there to cheerlead at our practices and games. Our relationship was about innocent hugs in the hallway and phone conversations after school, and I was so proud of our relationship and the fact that she wore my jersey at school. Having a relationship like that helped me feel like I was a normal sixth grader.

As my game time increased, so did media curiosity about me. It began with the local county newspaper and then escalated into a gigantic wave. An article written on the front page of the sports section in the *Atlanta Journal-Constitution* portrayed my family's life on a day-to-day basis and explained how I was able to play football. They photographed a game and shot a lot of pictures of my family at our home.

Then CNN decided to do a piece on me. They sent their cameras to the last game of the season, which was the muddiest game I've ever played in. After the game, I did a quick interview with them, even though I was totally soaked in mud from the tackles I made.

CNN decided they wanted to do a live interview to finish the piece. As a sixth grader in middle school, I was pretty nervous about going to the studio to do a live interview on one of the nation's largest stations. I hadn't done many interviews in the past, and this one was the most nerve-racking interview that I've ever done. I told my parents I felt like I was going to throw up, but they laughed at me and told me I'd be fine. Easy for them to say—they could sit and watch behind the scenes. I had to be on camera!

If my skin looked like I felt, it would've been about as green as the Collins Hill Eagle football jersey I was wearing. I felt fine immediately after the interview, and was elated to have the opportunity to share some of my experiences. It didn't strike me until later that millions of people were watching the show and were more than likely able to see right through my nervousness—so maybe I had something to be nervous about after all!

The final production turned out great, and I was thrilled by the response. Many people called or wrote to us just to say how they had been moved by the story. Reading the letters gave me a great feeling of accomplishment, because so many people said it had helped them. It made me think that all the work I put into improving myself on the football field was well worth the battle. I started to learn the joy of the unexpected rewards of hard work and dedication.

There were some other surprising opportunities that came along as more people heard my story. One of the stories found its way to the public relations director of the Atlanta Falcons. I was already a huge Falcons fan, but I became an extremist in 1997 when I was invited to the locker room before their game against their regional rival, the St. Louis Rams.

I met many of my football heroes and had the most unbelievable time at the game. My entire family was invited down onto the floor of the Georgia Dome to meet with Coach Dan Reeves before the kickoff.

I got to practice my butt roll against the best of the best as they had a good time messing around and getting to know me. Travis Hall was the Falcon's nose tackle, and I remember trying to model my playing style to be just like his long before I had the chance to meet him. Meeting him and the other Falcons inspired me to work harder still.

During the game, a few of the players had phenomenal performances. Jamal Anderson rushed the ball for over one hundred yards for the first time that season, and Ray Buchanan caught two interceptions in the Falcons' 34-31 victory over the Rams. They both gave me signed game balls, which I still cherish.

The NFL players just made me long for more competition. My own football season was over, but my father encouraged me to continue to weight train, so I could improve my strength and size for the next season, and so the offensive linemen would have less of a bulk advantage over me. But weight training was not football. I missed the contact, the tackling, the competing against others—and my father knew that I'd only be content if I was hitting someone like I was in football.

I needed an off-season sport where I could compete and fight. So my parents decided I should give wrestling a try. It meant competing against guys my own size. That was a new challenge, but I had no idea it would change my life.

Whenever I've faced adversity, I've used that challenge as motivation to win through, no matter the cost. When I meet with failure, I pick myself up, dust off the dirt from the fall and focus on trying again. You can't let failure beat you or give in to the temptation to take the easy way out. The world's greatest accomplishments aren't achieved on the first try.

CHAPTER 6 Passion for Wrestling

The sport of wrestling started out as a way for me to continue competing while I waited for the upcoming football season. It became my life's passion.

Wrestling wasn't the first idea I had, though. After the sixth grade football season ended, I wanted to try out for something else. I loved the teamwork, friendships, and competition of sports, so I tried to convince my dad that I could be a baseball player.

I pleaded with my father to play baseball, saying that because I could play so well with the neighborhood kids, I wouldn't have a problem playing for real. The Atlanta Braves were my favorite team, and the more I watched them play, the more I tried to convince myself that I could be just as dedicated and strong as those players.

Yet deep down, I knew that baseball was never going to be a sport where I would have an equal chance to compete with able-bodied athletes. I began to accept the fact that while I was able to excel in the context of football's physical contact, the sport of baseball demanded other skills beyond toughness—skills I did not possess.

Baseball wasn't the only sport I was interested in. I was an enormous hockey fan and a semi-experienced goalie after the countless street hockey games I played with my neighborhood friends. I was also a huge basketball fan, and I figured that it might be fun to play in a handicapped basketball league.

My parents were cautious and argued against trying out for these sports. They pointed out that I was too short to be an effective puck-stopper for an organized hockey team. And my father said just riding my wheelchair all around the basketball court wouldn't help me get in shape for the upcoming football season.

I now know that he just wanted to make sure I did well in whatever I decided to do, and he didn't want me to ruin my confidence after I had done so well playing football. He knew once I got the hang of the sport, I had an awesome time making the tackles, laying on a big hit, and playing with my friends.

My parents had seen me wrestle since I was a very young child and knew I had no problem taking people to the ground in football. My initial purpose when I began to wrestle, like so many other people that fall in love with the sport, was to get to be a better tackler on the football field. And I had the chance to compete against kids that were my weight now, and not kids who were twice my size.

I was eager to be a wrestler because I had been a fan of so-called "professional" wrestling for quite a long time. I liked those TV wrestlers because they always looked so strong and intense. I thought I'd actually get to jump off the top rope and body slam my opponents in the ring. Little did I know that the sport I was about to undertake was a different animal entirely.

Real wrestling is a completely different sport than the dramatic fighting seen on TV. It is one-on-one combat. It's the only school-sanctioned sport that, when you lose, it's because you got your butt kicked by another guy. That's a particularly hard thing to accept at a young age, but it is the kind of lesson that builds a tremendous amount of character; it's a character that comes with the sport.

I soon found out that on the mat, I was all alone. I didn't have ten teammates there to help me out if I made a mistake that I couldn't fix on my own.

As a former wrestler in Michigan, my father knew the sport would demand more out of me than I had ever put into anything before. When I decided to try to follow in his footsteps, I knew he was proud.

When my mom made a call to the high school's head wrestling coach, we were told it would be okay for me to come out and participate with the team. On my way to the first practice as a sixth-grader, I didn't feel the same amount of pressure I felt from the football tryouts only a few months before. I felt I had already proven myself to be a solid competitor and wasn't concerned about being cut from the team.

That first practice was brutal. I thought that I was in great shape from the football season, but I soon learned I was wrong. I decided that if I could survive a sport this grueling for one year, then I'd have no problem staying in great shape throughout the football season.

Our first exercise was running suicide style sprints up and down the wrestling mat. After we finished the first set of sprints, the coach, a volunteer who helped out the youth program as a feeder for the high school team, told us to catch our breath. We rested for 20 seconds before he told us to do another set of suicide sprints—but this time, we had to do a set of 10 push-ups at the end of every mat section.

I was already exhausted from the first set of sprints, but I wanted to make a good impression on the first day of practice, so I sprinted as hard as I could. It was refreshing to be able to run sprints without wearing 20 pounds worth of extra pads or a helmet. But then the coach told us to do a third set of sprints without any rest time, and I didn't feel refreshed at all.

When the sprinting torture stopped, the coach brought all of the young wrestlers into the center of the mat. He told us if we planned on sticking around for the whole season, we should expect to keep working just as hard. I'll admit that with that physical challenge, I was a little intimidated.

The youth coach went on to show us some basic wrestling moves, while the Collins Hill High School coach, Cliff Ramos, introduced himself to my father and me. He said he had spoken with my mother and was excited to help me become a successful wrestler. Coach Ramos told me he had been coaching for more than twenty years, and that he welcomed the new challenge of teaching me.

Wrestling is a conservative sport, in the sense that it never changes much. It's been around for so long, it's almost impossible to discover a new tactic or a move. People will change the same move countless times, but it's still the same move in the end. My case was different, though, because there were countless conventional moves that I'd rarely or never be able to use.

On that first day, Coach Ramos took my father and me to a corner of the wrestling room, while the rest of the team learned fundamental wrestling moves from the youth coach. He wanted to see the wrestling mat from my perspective, so he tucked his arms inside of his sleeves to get a better view of what I was capable of doing. He also wrestled around with my father using his knees and with his legs tucked into his pants.

Coach Ramos took on my training as a personal mission. In time, I found that very few coaches have Coach Ramos's level of knowledge to begin with, but even fewer have the patience to deal with a unique case like me.

I really didn't have an arsenal of tools to work with. We had to create entirely new techniques. When we first started to brainstorm, I only had two or three moves in my stash. But over time, Coach Ramos, my father, and I developed new techniques.

We did it through practice, by grappling on the mat together. Coach Ramos isn't the biggest guy in the world, but he can be a mean one. At the team's summer camps, we used to work together a lot. The other coaches would be off working with our team, and we had time to think of a ton of move sequences. I'd drill the same takedowns over and over while he critiqued the position.

From the beginning, he willingly devoted himself to helping me succeed. I look up to him because I believe wrestling has forged him into a man of strength and fortitude in life, not just in this sport.

I was just a kid out of sixth grade, and the head varsity coach at the high school was taking the time to help me two or sometimes three times a week. He told me one day I'd be able to compete in a match and defeat my opponent. And I believed him.

On the ride home my dad tried to explain that I would enjoy it even more once we got to wrestle in practice bouts. He told me my experience in wrestling and football would complement each other, because a perfect form tackle in football was no different than a wrestling takedown. I was excited about the new sport for a number of reasons, but especially because I was learning that in order to earn the right to be a wrestler, you had to be just plain tough. And that's exactly what I wanted to be.

At first, Coach Ramos concentrated on giving me counters to other wrestling moves, which meant I had to sit and wait for my opponent to make the first move on me. He wanted me to learn how to defend myself before I learned how to attack. He also invited me to watch—and even join in on—the high school practices he ran, where he coached one of the top teams in the state.

Watching the high school practice really opened my eyes to the intensity of the sport. I was blown away by the wrestlers' speed, balance, and strength; their ability to be so fast and still aware of their balance and weight distribution on the mat was like nothing I'd seen before.

The varsity wrestlers on the team had such an easy time dominating their opponents. The most important thing I observed from the varsity wrestlers was that they never stopped moving. Even when another wrestler scored a takedown against them, they kept moving.

I took that mentality into the practice room the next time I stepped onto the mat. Regardless of how few moves I was able to execute as a sixth-grader, I still realized the importance of movement and never stopping the flow of the match.

Other wrestlers in the practice room carried a lot more experience than I did when we began having practice matches. They could tower over inexperienced wrestlers like me because of their knowledge. They simply knew how to win, and I didn't.

The veteran wrestlers in the youth program destroyed every new wrestler they faced. As a new wrestler, I was upset by the fact that I could do nothing to keep these smaller practice partners from crushing me every time we wrestled. I felt like I was turning into their whipping horse, and I hated that feeling.

It wasn't just a matter of size. Every wrestler has to watch what he eats in order to make weight, because we have to weigh ourselves for the coaches so that the competitions are kept safe and fair. This actually gave me an advantage, because I was able to pack on more strength in a concentrated way. But strength, I learned, was not nearly enough to win in wrestling.

My father continually tried to assure me that I was no different from any other first-year wrestler, and it was only going to be a matter of time before I was the wrestler who would be taking on the bigger, but less experienced, kids. He told me that it was important for me to start wrestling at tournaments where I could get more experience with real matches than I ever could in the practice room.

I was eager for the chance to compete in my first wrestling tournament. When it came, I waited around with my dad for what seemed like the entire day. When the tournament volunteers finally called out the number of my first match, I felt an incredible rush of adrenaline and anxiety.

Because there weren't that many kids in our weight class, I had to wrestle with one of my teammates in that first match. He knew I was very inexperienced, but I wondered if he was as nervous as I was—after all, losing to me might be pretty embarrassing. It was my first match, and no one honestly believed I had a chance to win.

The match began, and before I could do anything, my opponent scored the first takedown to take the lead. I had known this match was going to be tough, but that kid was much faster than I anticipated.

I didn't have much of a game plan going into the match, but I wanted to hit the one move that I could do on a regular basis. That move was a counter to the most common wrestling move, a half nelson, where one hand is placed under the arm and behind your opponent's head to leverage him onto his back.

My objective was to wait for him to sink that half nelson in deep, so I could use my strong neck and shoulders to barrel roll him onto his back. I managed to do just that as he slipped a half nelson in around my neck. I exerted all of my strength to barrel roll him over, but somehow he was able to roll all the way around and flip me on my back.

I spent the remainder of my first wrestling match on my back, counting the lights and ceiling tiles. I knew I was going to lose, but I was still going to fight through it as best I could.

In order to pin your opponent, you have to hold both sides of his shoulders down on the mat at the same time. My neck had just spent the last few months carrying around a football helmet that weighed much more than my head. The helmet was extra tough to carry because I was on all fours at all times while playing football and had to keep my head up.

I knew my neck was my strongest point, so I just arched it the entire time to keep my back from getting pinned. Wrestlers call this "bridging." Whenever my opponent pressed me down on one side, the other side would pop up. He soon found that my neck was far too strong to be pushed all the way down for the pin.

After the match was over—and I lost—the tournament was too. I had waited eight hours with my dad to wrestle a single match. But even though I was disappointed to have lost my only match of the day, I was too excited with the thrill of competition to care much about the outcome. My body felt sore all over, and muscles were aching that I didn't even know I had.

In practice the next week, Coach Ramos took the time to help my dad and me brainstorm techniques we could try to get the most out of my abilities. It was clear that my limited counter style of wrestling wasn't going to cut it against any good wrestler.

Coach Ramos came up with a brilliant idea. He adapted my football barrel roll move for the wrestling mat, adding a shoulder lift. He called the move "the kelly," and it looked very similar to the way firemen pick up and carry unconscious victims.

I could use the move to rip apart my opponent's shoulder and score points while I was at it. It was ideal for my body type—a move that was specifically designed for a smaller, but stronger and stockier wrestler.

It didn't seem to help me too much in my next match though. The wrestler I faced had a much better technique than I did, and he ran through me by scoring more points than I was capable of defending against. He still couldn't pin me, and I took some pride in that, but the defeat was simply embarrassing.

I dedicated myself to working harder in practice, and honing my technique. One of the reasons I was losing, of course, was because I was wrestling guys who were much more experienced than I was. But in my third match, I had a realistic chance for a victory.

I was paired against a competitor who was equally as inexperienced. I was certain that this was my time, and that I'd get my first win. I felt like I won the match before I ever stepped out onto the mat—and that was my biggest mistake.

If I had mentally prepared myself in the way that I should have, if I hadn't let myself enter the match certain that I could defeat a less experienced wrestler, and if I had just worked that much harder, I would've had a great shot at winning.

Instead, I lost the match by a heartbreaking score of four to three.

It was a discouraging loss, and things only got worse from there. I went on to wrestle match after match and found disappointment each time I stepped in the center circle.

The defeat didn't let up at all, and my father grew just as frustrated with me as I was with myself. I felt like I was stuck in an endless cycle of losing. All I could see, feel, and taste was the empty bitterness of defeat.

My dad forced me out of bed several Saturday mornings before the sun was up to enter into tournaments that were often well over an hour or two away. As I continued to lose repeatedly, I started thinking about football in the fall, and what my friends were doing at home while I was being destroyed at these tournaments. I started to think that all this effort was pointless, and the thought that consumed me most was the end of the wrestling season.

I was now completely convinced that my dream of being a varsity wrestler was impossible. All I wanted to do was something that would be easier for me, like football or weight training. I couldn't handle the pain of constant defeat. I couldn't handle the fact that I just wasn't good enough to win.

I went through my entire sixth grade season without a single victory. I was ready to give up and quit.

If it wasn't for the advice of my father, I would've quit. I would've slunk away from the sport, completely defeated.

My dad told me for the first time he didn't win a single match in his first year either—which significantly motivated me at the time. His words gave me hope, because I respected my father as a man and for his obvious knowledge of the sport. In fact, it was only while writing this book that I found out my father had won several matches in his first year—he just lied to me to encourage me. I'd be upset about it, but it worked!

He told me I had to set a series of goals. I had to have some type of victory that I could realistically attain. At this point, I thought not getting pinned would be a great first year goal, and I had made that my objective in every match.

My father also told me something else that proved to be invaluable instruction. He noticed I was only wrestling as intensely as my opponent. That meant if my opponent was a slouch, I wrestled like one too. I did wrestle well against decent wrestlers and I stepped it up in those matches, but he saw that habit as a real weakness, and I knew he was right. I had to wrestle like a madman every second of every match, no matter how hard my opponent fought. I had to wrestle like the odds were against me—because they were.

Every single match I wrestled in sixth grade was on film. My dad captured every mistake I made on camera. When we went home after the tournaments, he would play the taped matches countless times, finding every mistake I made by slowing the VCR down to a crawl to pinpoint exactly where I went wrong.

I hated having the camera film me wrestling, because I was so pressured not to make the same mistakes twice. And whenever my dad found something blatantly obvious that he didn't like, we had to watch it over and over again. The worst came when I had to perform those messed up moves over and over again—with my dad as a sparring partner—until I got them right.

He taught me the most important lesson I would ever come to know through wrestling: wrestling is an individual sport. When you're on the mat, you're all alone. There's no teammate who can bail you out or pick up the slack. Nobody can change the fate of the match but yourself.

In the end, it was up to me alone to decide my fate and to walk out of the circle either defeated or victorious. I had to take the responsibility for winning entirely on my own shoulders, through my own preparation, determination, commitment, training, and skill. Others could help—others did help, invaluably—but in the end it was up to me. There could be no excuses.

It took a long time for me to realize exactly what was required to be successful in the sport. But the answers could be found in the wrestlers' work ethic. Dedication, desire and perseverance are the determining factors in a sport where athletic ability means less than intelligence, grit, and fortitude.

It was particularly hard to deal with these challenges right after finding vindication on the football field. Now I was getting my butt kicked all over the wrestling mat. I felt the frustration of my limits as an athlete, and facing those limitations took a lot out of me.

My family doesn't have many rules, but the most important one is that we never quit in the middle of a task or project once we've started. That meant if I wrestled in seventh grade, I'd have to finish out the entire year, even if I lost every single match once again. I didn't know whether I could handle that level of disappointment.

I would pray, asking God why He made me the way I am. I prayed that Jesus Christ would show me the right way to meet my challenges. I prayed for guidance as to whether I should continue wrestling the following year.

I believe God made me the way I am in order to show people that there is no amount of adversity that a single person cannot overcome if they fully trust themselves and trust in the will of Jesus Christ. And in time, I learned that I had to trust and believe in myself on the mat, and, even more importantly, I learned that I had to trust fully in the Lord my Savior, no matter the circumstances.

I would never have made the decision to continue wrestling in the seventh grade if it had been solely up to me. I didn't think I could compete, and I wanted to quit. It was my faith, the guidance of prayer, and my family that gave me the motivation, and ultimately the confidence, to return to the mat and try again.

It was the best decision I've ever made. I knew at the time that the decision would lead to a lot of sacrifices, but I never even imagined that, in the end, those sacrifices would yield the sweetest rewards of my life.

I prayed, and God delivered the answers. I may not have wanted to listen to those answers at the time, but I now know they were the answers He intended for me to hear.

The experience of wrestling is like no other. I know now that there is no challenge large enough to keep me away from where I want to be. I know I can solve any problem through learning and discipline. I know my limits, but never stop trying to break them.

CHAPTER 7 **Breakthrough**

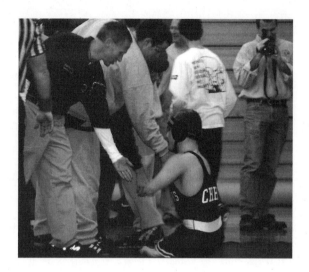

I was excited to start playing football again once the sixth grade wrestling season ended. Being down on all fours gave me a different, instinctual sense of the game, and I really started to miss the smell of the field before the season started.

I hoped the takedowns I learned from wrestling would help my tackling ability in football. After I had lost so many wrestling matches, I was excited to get back on the football field, where I knew I could destroy my opponents instead of serving as a human punching bag on the wrestling mat.

Football season continued to present the same obstacles that it had the year before, but practices seemed like a breeze in comparison to the level of intensity with which we had trained during the wrestling season.

I found that wrestling and weight training really did help me become a better football player. The other kids on my team were a lot larger than I was after they hit growth spurts in the summer months. But I had weight trained the entire summer, transforming weight from body fat to muscle, so I was a lot stronger than the year before.

The football season flew by. I was getting more attention from the media, and I enjoyed playing the game with my friends and team-mates, but I was getting less and less time on the field during games.

While I could wrestle as many matches as I wanted to, with football I had to rely on the coaches and their decisions about how much time I'd get in the games. If it was a close game, the odds were stacked against me.

I suffered a few nasty injuries in football that year. A very large and heavy linemen's sled was dropped straight on top of my right foot during one of the practices. Immediately, pain shot through my body, but I was determined to keep anyone from knowing, so I kept on practicing. I didn't want to give the coaches another reason to keep me off the field.

My dad finally noticed that I was hobbling around and putting a lot more weight on my left leg to compensate for the lack of stability in my right foot. It was pretty obvious that I was in a lot of pain by the time the team started to run sprints. After my father found out what happened, he made me sit out the next three practices.

Then I started repeatedly spraining my left foot. My dad had to tape the foot to make sure it was secure and stationary before every practice and game, or it would be wrecked from cleats smashing on top of it. I hated having to tape the foot all the time because I thought it meant I was weak and couldn't deal with the pain.

Even though I was determined to succeed, I believe the coaches saw me as more of an annoyance than anything else. And I was sick and tired of working so hard in practice everyday and not getting to play in the games. I didn't want to be a token player—I wanted a chance to prove that I could compete.

The reason I was playing less and less was because the other linemen were getting so much larger, and football had started to become a game based on size and not just grit. When I conceded this fact to myself, I started to miss wrestling. I had a feeling that once I wrestled again I might shock a few kids after all of the strength training I'd been working on.

My parents encouraged me to focus on the upcoming wrestling season. My mother wanted me to keep wrestling because she knew that my football days were nearly over. She knew that larger opposition meant I'd have to keep growing too, if I hoped to continue my football career and avoid injury. My dad promised me that I'd be shocked at how much I would improve from one year to the next, as I learned more wrestling skills. He helped me develop the mental confidence I needed to actually win a few matches the following year.

Once the football season ended, I immediately started practicing for the upcoming wrestling season. This time, I knew how intense the practices would be, and I planned on being ready.

The coach wouldn't let us wrestle in the first practice, so a few of us stuck around afterwards to grapple on our own. My friends from the season before didn't know what to expect, because I had grown to be a stronger and smarter wrestler. I was able to shut people down and frustrate them because they couldn't score as much as they were able to before.

I knew I wasn't a whipping horse any longer. So I couldn't wait to start the tournament season and see how I could do against real competition. It was one thing to do well in practice, but the feeling was completely different when I stepped onto the mat for a real match.

Coach Ramos kept me under his watchful eye and gave me a lot of support. He even started to send a few of the high school wrestlers over to the youth practices to teach the younger wrestlers. I can still remember feeling so much more motivated to push myself even harder when the high school wrestlers came to our practices. When we drilled, I took every chance to impress them by beating a few teammates.

I still felt the anguish from the season before, so I pushed myself in every practice, wanting to be in the best shape of my life before the first tournament.

The first tournament of the season pitted me against one of the toughest wrestlers in the state in my weight class. He was a scrawny and unimposing kid by appearance, but he was smart and athletic, and absolutely vicious on the mat.

I had no idea who he was, and I told my dad that I was going to "ruin him." My father wanted to keep me grounded and told me not to underestimate anyone, but he was glad to see the confidence I was building up. I didn't know he was a state runner-up from the year before, and a favorite to win the state tournament that year. In my ignorance, I had no fear.

I stepped onto the mat with a headstrong attitude, confident I was minutes away from my first victory. The first time we locked ourselves together, we realized it was going to be a fierce battle on both ends.

I tried to throw him in the first period, but he knew how to use his leverage. I lost my balance, and he took me to my back. I was familiar with fighting off of my back, but even without looking like it, he was stronger than anyone I had ever wrestled before.

I scrambled up off of my back and we stood facing each other in a standing position. Neither of us wanted to clinch up again and face the other's strength. He scored with a defensive-counter to a throw I attempted, notching five points for taking me to my back and holding me there without getting the pin. I got one point for getting up to escape to a standing position.

We continued to battle on through the duration of the match, but neither one of us could break past the other's defense. I ended up losing the match with a score of 5-1.

It was only after I had lost that I learned that this wrestler was one of the best in the state, and I wasn't surprised at all, after experiencing his grappling strength. This kid was a very good technical wrestler and had years more experience than me.

I was upset by the fact that I'd lost to such a weak-looking kid, but I learned a valuable lesson from it: no opponent should ever be judged from appearance. Every athlete has the potential to be the best at what they focus on, regardless of appearances.

Cael Sanderson is a wrestler from Utah who went on to wrestle at the University of Iowa State for the Cyclones. He was a four-time state champion in high school who had to work harder to be as successful in college. He's not the largest, strongest, or meanest-looking wrestler by any stretch of the imagination, but his other attributes make up for what he lacks in appearance. His speed, agility, and balance are simply phenomenal.

Sanderson went through his collegiate career with a record of 159 wins and 0 losses. He was a four-time NCAA champion and beat the previous win record set by Dan Gable. He went on to win a gold medal for the United States Olympic wrestling team in 2004 in the 185.5 pound weight class.

No one doubts Cael on the mat because he's a legend, and, in my opinion, the best collegiate athlete to have ever lived.

I don't just say that because I'm a wrestler and a fan of his, but because he is a role model with a truly amazing work ethic. He's my hero because I'm in the same boat as him, to a degree; people look at me and doubt my ability to wrestle and compete in the sport that I've grown to love so much. Sanderson proves that it's perfectly fine for an athlete to be an unassuming person, as long as you prove what you can do through competition, battling and winning on the mat.

People look at me and see limitations. I made the same error when I mistook my first opponent that season as nothing more than a skinny kid. Even though he was a very good wrestler, there is no excuse for losing a match to someone that I could have beaten if I had played a smarter game. My strength training had paid off to the extent that he was legitimately scared to lock up with me, but I made the mistake of judging the kid by his looks. I took a risky move to end the match fast—and it cost me.

That experience helped me understand how my different body type could be used as a psychological advantage to beat opponents. Every new match gave me the advantage of surprise. I needed to learn to not take it easy when the kids didn't know what to do against me, but to use that time to capitalize on their confusion. Maintaining my intensity for the entire match, I needed to be continually smart and aggressive, like a tiger stalking its prey.

It was a matter of physical stamina and drive, but also of mental strength, an equally important facet of the game. If I felt like my opponent was fatigued, I should take that time to push the envelope further and not let up for even a second. I would get inside his head, and he would start to see that it'd be a real battle if he had any hope of defeating me.

The match against the state runner-up opened a new door for me in my career as a wrestler. Even though the match ended up as a loss for me, I took more away from it than any victory. It proved to me, on reflection, that if I was smart and tough enough, I could defeat anyone I went up against.

I had learned from what I'd seen on the video tape. I wasn't one to go down quietly anymore, like I did as a sixth-grader. It was time to step out of the nicer frame of mind and adopt a nasty attitude on the mat.

Though I lost many matches in the next few tournaments, I was so close to my first victory that I could nearly touch it. I could feel the referee raising my arm in victory, I could feel my opponent's shoulders pinned to the ground, and I could feel the congratulatory backslaps of my teammates. I continued to lose matches because I continued to make mistakes, and that went on through half of my seventh-grade season.

However, I was closing the gap with each of my opponents. Sooner or later, I was going to have a breakthrough.

I continued gaining confidence by beating kids in practice, but my streak of losses continued for a year and a half—a total of 35 matches. The long stretch finally came to an end halfway through my second season, at the Gwinnett County Wrestling Championships, a tournament hosted by my team.

I took some time before the tournament started to look at the bracket sheets on the wall and see who my first opponent was. To my surprise, my first match was a forfeit because the kid was sick and couldn't wrestle, which put me automatically in the tournament finals without having to wrestle a single match.

It was quite a while before it was my turn to wrestle, so I waited with my friends and family in the stands. So many people I was close to came out to watch me wrestle—my parents, grandparents, aunts, uncles, cousins, sisters, and best friends. I knew I was not going to lose this time. It was a home match, and I had the overwhelming support of my family and friends in attendance.

When I walked down to the floor of the gym, I saw my opponent starting to warm up. He looked very nervous. I spoke with him before

I started my own warm-up, and he told me that he'd only been wrestling for couple of weeks and that this was only his fourth match.

I walked over to the other side of the gym to stretch out, and I silently thought to myself that this was it. It was time to break free of my doubts and have a good time dismantling this kid in front of my friends and family. I wasn't overconfident, but I was mentally geared for the match before I even stepped onto the mat.

There was fear in my opponent's eyes and I couldn't wait to capitalize on it. The signs of his trepidation were written all over his body. My ancestors, the Cherokee Indians, said that the enemy's weakness is our strength.

This wrestler was noticeably frightened when we came together at the center the mat. The referee blew his whistle, and we were under way.

The match was nearly over before it started.

I went after the kid with all my intensity and aggression, and he stumbled backwards trying to get away from me before I could get to his legs. I caught up to him and planted him in the rubbery mat.

I kept scoring by stripping him of his balance. He only delayed the inevitable by running around the edge of the circle, trying to stay away from me.

I gained a lot of confidence with each takedown I scored, and each time, I latched myself onto my opponent's body like a vice. My family was completely impressed and cheered every time I took the kid off his feet and flipped him in the air to score the takedown.

The match was a complete massacre. I finished my opponent off in the second period by scoring past the fifteen point mercy rule.

More than anything, I was shocked. I couldn't believe it had finally happened. I had won my first wrestling match! And I had done it because I was farther along the wrestling learning curve than my opponent—an advantage I'd never had before. But just as important, I was able to show what I had learned and prove to those who doubted my ability that I could do it.

I knew then that wrestling was a sport I truly wanted to conquer. There is something very beautiful about it. Maybe it's something that only another grappler could understand, but I feel that wrestling speaks to the deepest, simplest emotions of competition.

When a man steps onto the wrestling mat, he's only as good as his mind is strong. That's why wrestlers have to train the mind as hard as they train the body. In order to maximize your own potential, you have to realize that your mind—unless you work to reach a point of mental tenacity—will submit far sooner than your body.

I love wrestling because, in this sport, I am an equal. Inside the center circle, I have no weakness. My opponents are forced to expend just as much of their heart and soul to have the chance to beat me.

The beauty of a combat sport is that it's the only place where two competitors are only as good as their ability to take and dish out punishment. It's pure and unbridled competition on an even playing field that defies the boundaries people put between themselves.

Through my long year and a half of defeat, I stayed strong through prayer, family, and a willingness to sacrifice sweat and effort to meet the challenge.

It felt so good to stand on top of the podium and receive a first-place medal after all that losing, after letting down those around me. Immediately after the victory, I felt an explosion of love and relief from everyone who was there to support me.

The second half of the season had a tremendous finish—it was a mixture of wins and losses, but my confidence grew from both. My technique improved. I became more savvy and knew when to take risks to score. My endurance continued to soar as I pushed my body further in each practice and match.

The last two weeks of the season were the regional and state tournaments. In order to wrestle at the state tournament, I had to qualify by placing in the top four at the regional tournament. The tournaments were only separated by a week, and I desperately wanted to qualify for the state tournament.

I won my first match 7-4, my opponent's points coming only from escapes when I let him up. I fought my way through to the finals and then barely lost that match by a score of 1-0. It was a tough match, but I was pleased with the second-place finish at regionals because it qualified me for the state tournament.

I practiced hard for the next week with the rest of my teammates who made it to the state tournament along with me, but I ended up losing two straight matches at the tournament and being eliminated. Still, I felt it was quite an honor—and it was certainly a huge thrill—to make it to the state finals after my disappointing start.

It made me look forward to my eighth grade season all the more. In the off-season, I worked even harder in the weight room, and put on a lot more muscle mass. The extra strength and size helped when I decided to play football for the third and final year.

Other linemen on my football team outweighed me by well over twice my own weight, and the David and Goliath battle was beginning to get out of hand. My playing time kept falling, and so did my motivation, because my focus was now on wrestling. After my eighth grade season, I decided to stop playing football. I wanted to excel at wrestling, and while my playing time in football was steadily decreasing, my chances of being seriously injured were heading in the opposite direction. When I tackled people, I had to use my head to bring them down, and I'm fortunate to have never suffered a serious neck injury, since the competing players were so much larger than the year before.

As a true competitor, I wanted to be involved in a sport where I could be the dominant athlete. I didn't want to practice all week only to watch from the sidelines. With wrestling, my size couldn't stop me—only I could.

"The first period is won by the best technician. The second period is won by the kid in the best shape. The third period is won by the kid with the biggest heart."

— Dan Gable

CHAPTER 8

Rules, Moves, and Life on the Mat

Before we go any further in my story, I wanted to try and explain my sport to the non-wrestlers reading this book—about the lessons it teaches, the rules of the game, and some of the threats wrestling is facing in America today.

Outsiders don't realize that wrestling is a sport based on two pillars: sacrifice and smarts. The sacrifice comes from the intense training, effort, endurance, and toughness the sport requires. The smarts come from the techniques, mental focus, and psychological intimidation factor that champion wrestlers rely on.

If you have a very strong work ethic, there's no reason why you can't succeed in wrestling. In this sport, natural athletic ability is less important than absolute determination, grit, and knowledge. Sure, a great athlete with muscles and a competitive streak can thrive in this sport as much as in any other—but a wrestler with the same or less natural athletic ability can win if he's smarter and has the sort of drive that demands victory.

Tyler Parker, a teammate of mine, wasn't a natural athlete. He couldn't catch a football or dribble a basketball, but he had a greater work ethic, more intelligence, and was so technically sound at the sport that he became a four time state champion in Georgia. His senior season, he had only two offensive points scored against him— an amazing feat.

You can use a strong wrestler's strength against him, but it is almost impossible to defend against a mental edge. Every time you execute a move, the smarter wrestler will counter. It becomes a chess match: attack and counter, attack and counter. The smarter wrestler, the wrestler with the better technique, with the better inventory of moves, with the agility and mental toughness to keep coming at you, is the wrestler who will win.

It's a frustrating challenge to face a mentally tough wrestler. I've faced kids who weren't "A" students, but still have amazing natural ability—when they come onto the mat, they try to bowl me over. And I always beat them.

There was a kid from Marietta High School in Georgia who I wrestled five times over my career. He looked like a bronze statue, with a simply amazing physique. Yet I never lost to him. He was so intimidated the first time that he saw me, I beat him on a tapout—the only one I've ever seen. He always tried to use his strength against me, but then I'd get inside his head, try to take his balance away, and use his over aggressiveness against him. He was always so angry that he lost, he wouldn't even shake my hand.

Once you get through the initial learning curve—I was launched upside down and onto my head in one of my first wrestling matches because I didn't know what to expect—it becomes a game of hard mental and physical training, continual learning, and continual sweat. I am still learning about the sport on a daily basis, even after eight years of experience.

Once you train your mind as hard as you train your muscles, you will begin to notice how much more intensely you're able to push yourself. Training the mind should be your focus. The desire to improve yourself and reach peaks of mental strength that your opponent can only dream of achieving should consume you. When I practice, I work on being able to focus much more intensely when I'm fatigued and am trying to drive myself into my opponent's mind.

It doesn't always work. Once, I was in a submission wrestling tournament—which has a different set of rules from normal wrestling, but is still grappling for six to ten minutes—where I had to sit for hours, just hydrating and waiting. While I tried to keep focused, it was easy to let my mind wander as I talked to friends and teammates.

When I was finally called for a match, I had to refocus in order to win—barely. But then I had to wrestle another four matches in the space of little more than an hour. I hadn't done the right things nutritionally, so I felt like every carbohydrate had been drained from my body.

I made it to the finals, but was so physically drained that I lost my mental focus. I was convinced that I couldn't win. My mental edge dropped, and though I know I could've won the tournament with the right frame of mind, I lost in a real beat-down.

Mental focus is absolutely critical. I was talking to a kid at this same tournament, and we lost track of time. He had to go out to the mat cold, and he got arm-barred in short order—which I felt really guilty about afterward.

When I pull on my singlet and strap on my headgear, I turn everything else off. I put myself in a mental state where I can see what I need to, visualizing the course of the match and how I can defeat my opponent. The stakes are high; you can either win or be defeated in a way that strips you of every ounce of pride—because it's a sport where you can make no excuses. The competition is one-on-one.

Many former wrestlers succeed in achieving other goals thanks to the lessons they've learned from the sport. This includes many entrepreneurs who have credited their success to wrestling. A friend of mine, Jim Ravannack, has had amazing success in the energy industry. He had been a very successful high school wrestler in Louisiana, and he brought that same intense wrestling philosophy to the business world—finding a weakness, and exploiting it—in this case, in the market. And after finding enormous commercial success in the business world, he's helped young wrestlers by supporting youth programs and encouraging more kids to get into the sport.

Wrestlers are tough, but they're not braggarts, because they've been in the arena and have had humility pounded into them. They're united in the shared experience of knowing that if you let your guard slip for just a second, you lose. And every wrestler who's ever lived has been taken down, pinned, or otherwise beaten up in their career—even the best of the best.

Cael Sanderson, one of the greatest wrestlers of all time, has lost more than one match at the international level. He knew he couldn't rest on his laurels as the most successful collegiate wrestler. If he wanted to compete at the Olympic level, he had to redouble his training—and get past tough opponents—to be one of the best in the world. He lost a few matches along the way, but like all champions, his losses only made him stronger because he learned from them. He ultimately won the gold medal he sought.

Wrestling creates a brotherhood unlike anything else. Older wrestlers remember opponents they faced decades ago. They can talk about old matches with the same amount of detail as if they happened yesterday. Wrestlers never forget. The experiences are too intense.

The night before one tournament, my father ran into someone he had wrestled against in middle school. After talking to each other for a few minutes, they recognized each other from one match way back in middle school—the only match in which my father had been pinned. Even almost thirty years later, the experience was still fresh in his mind—he could tell me everything that happened, as well as how it happened.

The brotherhood of wrestling includes many success stories. The canon of former wrestlers includes eleven former U.S. Presidents, such as George Washington, Abraham Lincoln, and Dwight D. Eisenhower.

Dennis Hastert, our current Speaker of the House, and Donald Rums-feld, our Secretary of Defense, were both very successful collegiate wrestlers. Other famous wrestlers include Tom Cruise, Robin Williams, Jay Leno, Bill Maher, Harvey Keitel, Vince Vaughn, John Belushi, and Ashton Kutcher to name a few. Few people are aware that a couple of very talented musicians like Maynard James Keenan of Tool and A Perfect Circle, Layne Staley of Alice in Chains, Garth Brooks, and Ludacris were all tough wrestlers.

Wrestling doesn't merely teach the principles of good athletics and facing challenges in terms of sports and competition—it also teaches you to form common bonds with your teammates and friends, to support others, and to never accept fear or defeat. As Frank Herbert, one of my favorite sci-fi authors, wrote: "Fear is a mindkiller."

One of the most important lessons wrestling has taught me is humility. If you aren't at least a little nervous before every competition, you aren't human. The key is working past that, and reaching the point where you can focus on what you have to do in order to win.

We're not as invincible as we often think we are. Injuries are always possible in this sport, just as much as they are in football. And wrestlers also have to watch what they eat in order to make weight. They have to know how much to train in order to stay in top shape. They have to stay away from anything that will taint their body's condition.

Wrestlers learn through the bad experiences on the mat as well as the good. It's a lot like learning that fire is hot by putting your hand in it. Sometimes, it's the best way to learn.

Because of the values that wrestling instills, the sport can make an enormous impact on kids: keeping them clean, strong, disciplined and motivated. The great Iowa State University wrestling coach, Bobby Douglas, is now known as the coach of Cael Sanderson. But the path Coach Douglas followed to success is one that speaks to the real impact of wrestling.

Douglas grew up in southern Ohio at bus stop number thirty-two, living in horrible poverty. He was in an impossible circumstance and was given nothing from the day he was born. But through the dedication and hard work he learned from wrestling, he became the very first black wrestler to win an Ohio state championship. And as a coach, he brought an unranked Arizona State team to an NCAA championship.

Coach Douglas says that he'd be dead if it weren't for wrestling. The sport kept him off the streets and, more than that, made him an American Olympian. He's one of the few wrestlers to ever beat Dan Gable. Because of his experience, Coach Douglas is a believer in the idea that wrestling can work miracles in the lives of young men.

I've seen this principle myself. I've seen young wrestlers in poor urban communities who, because of wrestling, make the choice to stay away from drugs and finish their education—and continue to compete—instead of falling down a wayward slope like so many of their peers. They have gained the character necessary to do this because of the discipline wrestling demands.

Wrestling groups such as Beat the Streets that reach out to kids in these communities produce amazing results. Joe Williams, a young

man from Chicago, even became an American Olympian after starting out in one of these programs.

The kids that I've met through working with these foundations
are always eager to see someone demonstrate a move, to talk about life
and wrestling, and to learn the lessons of the mat. And I know these
lessons have an impact on their lives well beyond just sports—helping
them say no to drugs and take the right course in their lives.

Groups like Beat the Streets help kids by giving them the tools
they need to wrestle—they provide funding for headgear, mats,
Gatorade, and training equipment. But most of all, they inspire.

Yet the shocking fact is that competitive wrestling is actually on
the brink of extinction in the United States—by act of Congress.

THE THREAT OF TITLE IX

Certain legislation, which began with well-intentioned people
who just wanted to bring about equality, has caused the sport of
wrestling to suffer tremendously. Since Title IX was passed in 1972, the
General Accounting Office reports that over 170 men's wrestling programs have been eliminated.

Title IX is an equal opportunity act that has helped countless
women across the country afford to go to college because of expanded
athletic scholarship opportunities. The downside to Title IX arises
from the fact that it requires an equal split in any given school's scholarship funds between men's and women's sports and teams.

Here I am at age 12,
playing football for
Collins Hill.

Age 10, caving in southern Indiana with the cub
scouts. My Dad is on the far right, and Grandpa
Norm is standing next to him.

Having fun at age 12 with my sisters.
Amber is on the left and Lindsay is
on the right.

LEFT: Easter egg hunt with the family at age 15.

BELOW: Age 12, meeting Atlanta Falcons Long Snapper Adam Schreiber before a football game vs. the St. Louis Rams.

Wrestling in my Senior year.

Wrestling in my Sophomore year against my friend Brooks Tait. My final winning match at the State tournament was against him.

At the Arnold Classic, March 2005, prior to breaking the record for the modified bench press of 360 pounds. This is how I look when I get focused.

ABOVE: Riding horses at my Uncle Matt's house in Michigan.

LEFT: Age 16, playing around with my sisters Lindsay and MacKenzie and our puppy, Sandy.

ABOVE: Here I am driving my Cherokee.

ABOVE RIGHT: At the ESPY Awards in July 2004 with Coach Cliff Ramos.

RIGHT: The GNC Show of Strength in Atlanta, Fall 2003, with fitness legend Dave Hawk.

Senior Prom, 2004. My best friend, Joey Leonardo, is on the far left.

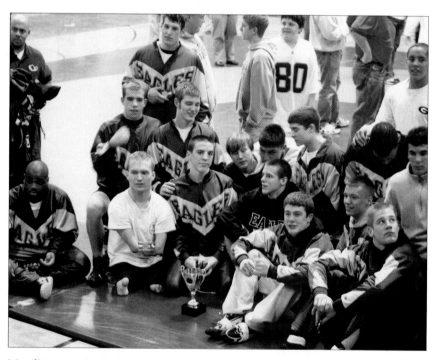

Wrestling team picture, Senior year, 2004.

This is how I do shoulder raises.

Here I am with "The Governator."

On the Larry King show.

University of Georgia wrestling team, January 2005.

Family picture, Spring 2005. Left to right, Mom, Lindsay, Me, Amber, MacKenzie, Dad.

Generally, many more men than women want to compete in collegiate sports, so men's sports have to share a much smaller financial pie. The result is that less money is given to help smaller programs, sports that don't bring in as much revenue or school recognition as football, basketball, or baseball.

It's a profoundly unjust situation, and one that unfairly penalizes many inexpensive men's sports activities. Small athletic programs such as men's wrestling, soccer, lacrosse, swimming, and gymnastics have suffered because the larger football and basketball programs have much more money allocated towards them. It's a problem that's spreading across the country, and one I've experienced personally and through my friends.

In the SEC, there are no Division I men's soccer teams, despite the fact that it's one of the biggest high school sports in the South. Trevor Garner, a friend and roommate, was a four year letterman in soccer and valedictorian of his high school, but unfortunately because he wanted to go to school in-state, he had to give up playing the sport he loved.

The University of Georgia, my own school, dropped its wrestling program in the early 1980s, and the SEC hasn't had any wrestling opportunities for many years. There are simply no scholarship opportunities for a wrestler in Georgia. Wrestlers at my college can continue to participate in the club level, but we're unable to wrestle in NCAA sanctioned tournaments, because the program was cut off.

The wrestling team at the University of Georgia has to share their mats with break-dancers and other groups—the mats are damaged as a result, and leaving sand, dirt, hair, and germs that can cause ringworm and other skin ailments in wrestlers. Because many colleges don't take the sport seriously, wrestlers are forced to practice at bizarre hours.

Wrestling is a relatively low cost and low maintenance sport, and wrestlers themselves are usually intelligent and on academic scholarships. Colleges and universities can take simple steps to respect wrestling as a sport, and treat those who play it with respect as student athletes. But absent any public pressure or incentive to do so, many programs will just die off.

The only saving grace for wrestling right now lies in its appreciation in the midwestern states and the development of new women's collegiate wrestling programs. The 2004 Olympics marked the first year that women were able to wrestle in the Olympics. Midwestern schools like Northern Michigan, where my friend Mary Kelly wrestles in the 105 pound weight class, have used women's wrestling programs to justify restarting their men's programs. My hope is that the development of women's wrestling as a sport will help revive collegiate wrestling for men.

I strongly support women's sports, and I don't believe we should put one dollar less towards women's scholarships. And I believe that Title IX has done some good things to enhance the opportunities women are presented with in America, but there is simply no reason why it should have to harm other men's sports. As Jessica Gavora, the author of *Tilting the Playing Field: Schools, Sports, Sex and Title IX,* writes: "A law designed to end discrimination against women is now causing discrimination against men."

There is a growing movement for Title IX reform, motivated by athletes, coaches, and parents who've had enough of the unfair system. For those of us who care about wrestling, we need to develop a greater appreciation for the character building aspect of the sport if wrestling is going to survive past the century. We need to build a greater awareness about the unintended consequences and dangers of Title IX in order to save wrestling and the other college sports that the biased legislation affects.

The sport of wrestling has had a monumental impact on countless lives, and I have no idea what my life would be like if wrestling wasn't such a big part of it. If I had never been forced to give up wrestling because of a government quota system, I would have had the chance to show my abilities on the mat at the NCAA level, to reach out to people and prove to them that anything is possible.

THE RULES OF THE GAME

Of course, to win, I had to learn to maximize my ability within the confines of the rules of wrestling. So I should probably say a little bit about the rules and how I adapted to them.

The easiest way to understand the sport of wrestling is to simply watch it. But here's a breakdown of how points in a match are earned. There are three periods to a wrestling match. In the first, both wrestlers are standing. In the second and third, one wrestler is crouched on all fours as the other wrestler kneels behind him, gripping his opponent on the elbow and around the waist.

A pin, where both shoulders are held down against the mat, is like a knockout in boxing. It is the best way to end a match early. It can happen at any point, regardless of the score in the match, and is an automatic win.

But matches are often won and decided by the wrestlers who score more points than their opponents. You can't walk out on the mat and expect to pin anyone right away. You have to fight for it, and anything can happen at any point in time during the match.

The first and most common way to score is by a takedown, which results in scoring two points. During my senior season, I had close to one hundred takedowns. The takedown is scored when one wrestler establishes a dominant position on the top of another, and it usually happens when a wrestler can control his opponent's legs or manage to throw or hurl an opponent onto the mat.

People would take me down by pushing down on my head, and then preventing me from raising my arms to defend myself as they moved around behind me. I use the takedown method of scoring most often, as it's the most fluid and natural. My favorite takedown method is basically a backstroke motion from all fours as my opponent presses down on my head. I can use my leverage to lock onto my opponent's hips and flip behind him to get two points with the move, called a "peak-out" or "short duckunder."

The second most common way to score comes from escapes, where the wrestler in the bottom position is able to get away and free their body to start in the neutral standing position again. One point is awarded to the escaping wrestler.

Escaping from the bottom position is always my first objective. When the whistle blows, I'd try to leverage my opponent off my back and get into a standing neutral position to try for a takedown. Many wrestlers can easily escape from me, because my limbs prevent me from keeping their hips in place.

Next is the reversal, which is another way to free oneself from the bottom position. In this scenario, the wrestler on the bottom switches position and moves to the dominant position on top. Two points are awarded to the wrestler securing the reversal.

I didn't excel at reversals unless I was on the bottom looking for an escape and could execute one of my favorite moves, the "Gramby" roll. It basically looks like a sideways somersault. But I would have to do it quickly in order to catch my opponent off his guard.

The final way to score points involves the wrestler in control pinning one of his opponent's shoulders to the mat. This is called a "near fall." The fall is another way of saying pinned, but that only happens when both shoulders are locked down simultaneously. The near fall points are awarded when one shoulder is held down, but both can't be at the same time. This is worth two to three points, depending on how long the wrestler is held on their back.

In my own case, I've had the ability to arch my neck in order to avoid being pinned, but I'd give up near fall points as wrestlers were able to hold me on my back. I'm always looking to get a pin and hold a wrestler on his back (and end a match early), but I find that a lot of times, I'm able to win through near fall points. It prolongs the match, but in the end I usually come out on top. The best outcome, of course, is to achieve an early win, so that I have a real physical advantage—because I'm fresher—for the next round of the tournament.

Even if you score a great deal more points than your opposition, you still have to hold onto your defensive foundations in order to stay out of trouble; trouble that puts you in a position to get pinned. It doesn't matter what the score is, because once one wrestler pins the other, the match ends immediately.

I lost many matches early in my career, but I've never been pinned. Like a boxer who's never been knocked out and always tries to avoid that, protecting yourself from being pinned can cause other mistakes and make you give up points. But it has also allowed me to fight until the last second of each match with every ounce of energy I've got inside.

The little things Coach Ramos noticed in my wrestling technique were very important in improving my abilities. I didn't need to come up with fifty different moves if a series of five would work well enough to get the job done.

One of my personal favorite moves was one I did accidentally, but I knew I had discovered something when I felt the guy wince when I hit it. Afterwards, I asked coach if he knew what I had done, but he didn't have a clue either. It took an hour or two of experimentation after the match to find the move again, but it was just as lethal the second time I tried it. Coach Ramos called the move the "Jawbreaker" and we were both immediately shocked by how effective it was.

It was more of a jaw-clamp than anything else. I'd jam the end of my arm into the hinging-point of the jaw line. The wrestling move inflicted so much pain that some kids would roll on their backs in an act of submission to make it stop. I was the only one able to pull off the move to its full potential, because I trained to squeeze my arm muscle with the butterfly press. I've had kids tell me that, after the Jawbreaker, they couldn't eat normally for a week.

Coach Ramos was so excited about discovering the Jawbreaker that he had me test it out on other coaches. I think he got a kick out of helping me rough-up his peers. Coach Ramos is at least partially responsible for my "glutton-for-punishment" attitude, because he's given me physical fits in the past. The rest may have to lie on the shoulders of my rough ancestors out of Scotland, Ireland, the Southern United States, and the Cherokee nation.

One of the main reasons I've found lifelong success with wrestling is because I've taken the necessary steps to be physically prepared. When I face another kid, I know that he had to make weight at the same time I did and it's not easy to temporarily strip your body of nutrients and expect to perform at the highest level.

Don't blame your exhaustion on a lack of sleep if you choose to abuse your body with a bad diet, lack of exercise, or general inactivity. There are a number of problems, of which sleep may be one, that directly affect your body's capacity to operate at the highest efficiency. One of the key issues that wrestlers have to address is their weight.

Wrestlers cut weight for two main reasons: their coach requests them to for the sake of the team, or they need to avoid an opponent that they haven't had any luck defeating. Kids are very rarely affected by the weight loss because you lose the extra pounds by sweating off water weight. You can then replenish the water weight and hydrate yourself before you step onto the mat, and your opposition can do the same.

There are sad cases where kids have cut too much weight, as in any sport with weigh-ins, and have had negative health ramifications. It's usually the younger wrestlers who are curious about the sport but proud to be involved, who want to show off how much weight they're cutting. Usually it's only a trivial amount of weight they're trying to lose, and they only want attention from other kids at school to recognize they're wrestlers. So instead of toughing it out and not attracting attention to themselves, they want to look cool and walk around school spitting in a cup to lose less than a tenth of a pound.

The easiest way to cut weight is to wear a lot of extra clothes and just run until you get a good sweat going. You can wrestle around to lose the weight too, but that's difficult when you can't eat too many carbohydrates to keep you going.

Before nationals in my senior year, I had to cut about 17 pounds of weight to fit in the 103 pound weight class, after I was up over 120 pounds for the state tournament. In order to lose extra weight, I tried to drink as much water as I could and cut down on food intake. As the tournament approached, I cut back on fluids and balanced my exercise schedule. I had to wrestle with my coach up until the last moment to make weight, but I did it.

That experience was tough enough to make me appreciate good food—Christmas and Thanksgiving come right in the middle of a wrestling schedule, and no red-blooded American wrestler wants to suffer through those times with a half a slice of turkey as their holiday meal.

Many of my wrestling teammates and I would watch the Food Network longingly during the season, writing down the recipes and dreaming of the days when we could eat whatever we wanted. We'd hold onto these meal ideas for months as we had to watch our weight. Some of us—I won't say who—would gorge ourselves after the final tournament on Cheetos, Doritos, and, best of all, multiple cans of Funfetti icing.

Weight-cutting can have negative consequences in performance and health, but when done correctly, it's a part of the sport that helps you achieve a physical balance. I know my family prefers it when I'm not cutting down on weight, because I'm a lot less irritable when I can eat and drink whatever I want.

I've always wrestled better when I cut weight, because it makes me faster. At first, until my sophomore year in high school, it was easy, because I only wanted to cut a pound or two. After that, weight cutting not only made me faster, but because the process honed my discipline, it gave me a lot more personal investment in the matches.

Weight cutting always enhanced my focus too. If I was focused on making weight after I left the practice room for the day, I'd be more likely to concentrate on my matches after the weigh-ins in the morning. I've felt no greater satisfaction in my life than knowing I've sacrificed my body through weight cutting, practiced as intensely as I could everyday in preparation for a six minute match, and fought as if my life depended on it to come out on top.

It's worth clarifying that weight-cutting doesn't deserve some of the negativity that it gets. There are tons of ridiculous myths and glorious legends surrounding wrestling that people ask me about. Extreme weight cutting is one of them. Others include deadly cases of ringworm, bone snapping slams, and inflating the dangers of cauliflower ear.

In eighth grade, I had one of my only encounters with ringworm, a communicable fungus that looks like a mosquito bite and incubates in some wrestling rooms. It was right in the back of my head, and made me go bald in a spot roughly the size of a nickel. After it was treated, my hair grew back, and I haven't had another problem with it—but the experience definitely made me a clean freak. You can understand why I showered and cleaned myself off immediately after practice from then on out.

Cauliflower ear is another physical issue related to wrestling that's often misunderstood. This condition occasionally happens when the cartilage in your ear separates during the intensity of a match, and scar tissue forms as the cartilage condenses on it. In the context of the wrestling world, this is viewed an indication of sacrifice and dedication, the badge of a grappler—you don't want to scrap with a guy who has a cauliflower ear.

The outside world views it differently, of course. I once teased a girl by saying that cauliflower ear was contagious—it's not. But that's why wrestlers wear headgear, to prevent that sort of thing.

Now as to why wrestlers wear those singlets—just remember that it's about function, not form, so it has a lot in common with the standard outfit for a gymnast. The traditional latex singlet is really the best way to avoid breaking fingers or toes by getting them caught in clothing. Because I wrestled in a lower weight class, some people expected me to wear a smaller singlet—but my torso is a normal size for a 180–200 pound man, so I had to wear a larger one. Some wrestling teams are moving away from the singlet, and in open tournaments, many wrestlers will wear bike shorts or Under Armour.

Wrestling is also sometimes given a bad name because people don't understand or don't accept the fact that two people could possibly desire to put themselves in harm's way in order to truly test their ability to handle tense situations.

Wrestling takes a lot of heat from people who talk badly about the barbaric aspect of the sport, but there are so many life-changing lessons the sport teaches to anyone who participates and hangs in through the tough times. People tend to ignore the fact that the sport has the same martial art value as any type of karate. Kids and adults can participate and learn the same lessons at their own pace just like most other martial arts.

In fact, as one of the first five Olympic sports, wrestling is considered the very first martial art. Actually, you can trace wrestling back to the ancient books in the Bible. In Genesis 32, Jacob wrestles with God, and when he prevails, is renamed Israel. While there probably weren't any referees around to see it, this is probably the first instance of what we know as modern wrestling.

Wrestling was originally a part of what is now called "Pankration" by the Greeks. They used it as one of five ways to test for the perfect warrior in the first Pentathlon. Wrestlers used their skills to throw much larger opponents than themselves and it became a popular sport to place wagers on. To avoid confusion with who the spectators were betting on, wrestlers wore different colored belts. The wrestlers wearing the white belts were said to have stained them yellow with sweat, dyed them green with grass stains, and eventually discolor them brown with dirt.

The darker the belt, the more experienced the grappler. This is why modern martial artists wear the different colored belts as a symbol of their level of accomplishment. I'm involved in a movement to bring belts back to wrestlers as a way to show an athlete's devotion to one of the most effective martial arts of all.

Only boxing and mixed martial arts competitions offer the same solutions to a warrior spirit like wrestling does. When two individuals step into the boxing ring, fighting cages, or center circles of wrestling mats, they are aware of the fact that they are in for a war. Each one of these combative but life-changing sports demands the kind of total commitment only individual sports can.

I am thoroughly impressed with Tiger Woods' ability to stay in such a mentally focused state of mind and be so consistent on every golf course he plays. Even though golf isn't a game where one's physical power is set against another's—at least not to the extent it is in wrestling—Tiger still displays the tenacity and indomitable will necessary to succeed anywhere in life. I'm sure he would've made a great wrestler with his attitude.

Wrestlers have to stay optimistic. Because there are a limited amount of variables and moves, we have to stay focused on what we do well. We have to hold on to our resiliency and answer any critic through our actions on the mat.

There have been so many times throughout my career when I've reached out for a takedown, but came up less than an inch away from locking and pulling my opponent's leg towards my body. Even though I was so close to securing those takedowns, I never made excuses except for the excuse those lost attempts gave me to work harder.

I consider my hard work and intensity in the practice room an advantage I hold over my opponents. I visualize how hard they're working in the practice room, and I push myself that much harder.

I will never come into a match unprepared and in a worse cardiovascular condition than the kid I'm up against, because that is an advantage I can't afford to give up. No matter what the score is in the third period, I always have the chance to drive my challenger that much harder with every second.

If he can't stay at my pace, then he's going to be in for a beating as the match carries on. It only gets tougher to keep yourself at the same intensity level for the duration of a six minute match, but I've always had the ability to take myself to new heights of effort as the match continues to progress.

I might be disadvantaged to a degree because, if my opponent stands far enough away, it's hard for me to pursue him and take him down. But I can embarrass him by pushing the pace and driving him off the mat.

If my cardiovascular shape is better than his, then there's no reason why I can't push the level of intensity for the entire match and drive myself harder than him. I also work hard to keep a mental and technical edge in aspects of the sport, so I'm able to better anticipate my opponent's moves, counter them, and derail his gameplan.

Another advantage I have over opponents is the fact that many of them who haven't wrestled me before will underestimate me before the match begins. They soon think differently once we get underway, but there's a window of opportunity I have before the kid is able to recognize that I'm not out there for show. He needs to be prepared if he's going to have a chance to stand in and exchange moves and counter-moves with me. If the wrestler hasn't felt my strength yet, then he isn't aware that I can move and score fast, before he's able to react with his game plan.

I love when kids believe they can charge in and try to flip me over on my back. They're shocked at my strength—the product of hard weight training—and they're frustrated and confused because they have to change their tactics on the fly while I'm charging into their legs.

I always try to stay positive and not worry about the disadvantages that I face, because hard work will overcome any physical difference I have from my opponents.

There are a number of things that I'm not able to do as a result of not being able to reach too far and grip onto any part of the kid's body unless they get close enough. Smarter wrestlers decide to stay away from my body and try to avoid the grappling aspect of the match by pushing down on my head and keeping their distance away from my body.

It's very frustrating to rush another wrestler all over the mat and have the referee sit back and not intervene to force him into action. Technically, this is stalling—and the referees should call it, but often don't.

My opponents score takedowns most often by pushing down on my head to keep me from grappling with them. From that position, they try to spin around to my back. Then they'll let me up and score their two points for the takedown and give up the one point for the escape because they don't want to stay on the mat with me for long, at which point my upper-body strength could then come into play.

I call that tactic "dancing," because it looks a whole lot more like that than a typical wrestling stance. But it's only one of the many obstacles I have to contend with. I can't get a good grip on my opponent's body without using my armpit or chin to lock one of their limbs in with my shoulder. It makes it nearly impossible to get any type of grip on anyone when the kids continue to avoid me by dancing and spinning around behind me.

I've worked with a lot of coaches to try to figure out how to stop that from happening, but against a fast opponent, it's a difficult thing to prevent. My strategy has to be to hinder their ability to score the easy points and to force action near the center of the mat where they can't run away from me.

A couple of times, I've even gone so far as to use a move Coach Ramos named the "rope-a-dope," which involves me laying one shoulder down on the mat to entice the kids to jump on top of me to try and get the pin.

It's worked, to a degree, at times—but even then, the kids are nervous about coming in and actually wrestling. Or they're wise enough to know that even while I'm lying on my back and daring them to come down and press the other shoulder down for an apparently easy pin, it's a trap. An intelligent game plan by my opponent will lead him to avoid taking that bait.

My opponents frequently try to get me in a front head lock, and then move to shuck me to one side or the other. As I've moved into submission wrestling since high school, other moves like the guillotine or triangle chokes are used against me. But I've always believed that the physical disadvantages that I have can be wiped away as long as I keep my focus throughout the entire course of the match, making the commitment to work as hard as I can in preparation for each time I step out there.

Wrestlers are also taught to keep both of their eyes fixed on their opponent's hips. The body can't move or be deceptive in any way without the hips following along. If a wrestler keeps a close eye on his opposition's hips, he'll put himself in a much better position to defend against any attack. Conversely, staring at an opponent in his eyes will only allow him to be deceptive enough to score an easy takedown. Great wrestlers avoid eye contact.

In a live wrestling match, the hips are the only way to definitely know where your opponent plans on going without the ability to juke you out and score without much of a fight. Watching your opponent's hips affords you an opportunity to prepare for anything he might throw at you.

Good wrestling coaches teach their athletes to control their opponent's head. The head will follow wherever the body goes, and the neck is a weak muscle to attack in comparison to struggling against the biceps or quadriceps, which is why wrestlers work so hard to strengthen their neck. Getting control of your opponent's head is an easy way to pull him off balance and bring him down to the mat hard. The most brutal throws are usually done that way.

It's very advantageous for one wrestler to pull their opponent's head away from the center of the body, because it causes that wrestler to be off-balance and one can score a quick takedown. Olympic champion Cael Sanderson controls his opponent's heads so well that he's able to take the best competition in the world off balance and score.

I love wrestling more than nearly anything else in my life, and I will do anything to achieve greatness in it. I love being part of a community that truly understands passion for a sport, and carries triumphs proudly through stories that we will remember for the rest of our lives. And I love the fact that the sport has had a positive impact on the lives of millions of families, fans, and wrestlers around the world—including me.

In life and in competition, good character is the foundation of everything. We build our character by taking chances, accepting challenges, and helping others meet their goals. This is not just a good idea- it's a way of life.

CHAPTER 9 **Going for Varsity**

103 Maynard	145 Richard
112 Parker	152 Schieber
119 Bui	160 Quintero
125 Patrick	171 McGuire
130 Lukacs	189 Gauthier
135 Whittington	215 Canova
140 Nash	275 Thomas

COLLINS HILL
Wrestling

fter going a year and a half without a victory, I was on a one-win streak, and I wasn't about to stop there. I was determined not to make the same mistakes that I had the previous thirty-five times. That attitude, coupled with an improved training regimen, allowed me to qualify for the state tournament by the end of my second season as a seventh grader. I lost both of the matches at state that year, but it was a great accomplishment for me to get that far.

I was determined to come back as a much stronger wrestler in the eighth grade. I weighed 75 pounds during the end of my season, but I was a solid 20 pounds heavier the following season. I had chosen to leave football behind, but I was excited to improve myself as a wrestler in anyway that I could.

My new focus on wrestling had an immediate impact. In my eighth grade season, I won almost every match I wrestled in leading up to the state tournament. I was playing loose and wrestling smart. I had gotten much stronger than the season before—so much, in fact, that I sometimes made the mistake of trying to overpower everyone I wrestled without using the proper technique.

My family and my coach were excited to see how eagerly I competed now that I was a force to be reckoned with. No one was taking matches with me lightly, and if an opponent beat me, it was always a hard fought match he deserved to win.

I worked hard to prepare for that season by going to as many camps as I could and by lifting weights almost everyday. I grew tremendously as a person and as an athlete, but more importantly, I was ambitious enough to immediately set a new goal after having conquered the last. I had a great time wrestling now that I was winning, but that wasn't enough—I made it my goal to become a state champion.

In the end, I was the county and regional champion during my eighth grade season. I wrestled so well that I hoped to be the number-one contender for the youth state title. I was convinced there was no reason why I couldn't be a state champion after I felt the taste of accomplishing something great by qualifying for the state tournament at such a young age.

While I wasn't able to win the state championship in my eighth grade year, I had a decent performance at the state tournament. I was pleased, but not satisfied, with my technical execution, and I realized that while becoming a state champion was my dream, I knew it was going to take a lot more work than I'd already put in to make that dream come true.

The added challenge was the next year, when I graduated to the ninth grade and became a high school wrestler. I'd have to face much more difficult competition, though I'd also have the chance to work with Coach Ramos and the varsity wrestlers every day.

Collins Hill High School is one of the largest schools in the southeast. There were more than 3,500 students in attendance during my freshman year. The Eagles were known for their tough sports teams and great teachers. I was fortunate enough to have my uncle, Coley Krug, as my high school principal during my freshman and sophomore years.

Like most kids, I was very self-conscious during the first few days of high school. The halls seemed like a labyrinth, the teachers talked too fast, and the other students were curious about me but too worried about my potential reactions to ask. I remember going into the cafeteria to eat lunch on the first day and wondering where I was going to sit. It's a situation that every kid faces, and it doesn't get any easier when you're in a wheelchair.

I had skated through middle school with A's in almost every class, but I hit a wall as a teenager and began to realize that high school required a lot more work. The faster pace of high school lectures made it hard for me to keep up with the rest of my classmates and write down notes.

My parents suggested I use a tape recorder to capture every class lecture and write the notes down later, but it was only a matter of days before I completely abandoned the recorder. I was so sick of having to listen to each class twice that I decided I'd rather learn to take notes down fast.

It was even difficult to finish the tests in the allotted time because they were nearly all essay based exams. I had a lot of difficulty adapting to writing at a fast pace and not running out of time. But for all the new challenges, I excelled in other areas. I gradually made new friends, and wrestling helped me to establish close relationships with new people.

I gave myself new goals in the physical arena. I worked out an arrangement with our assistant head wrestling coach, Jim Tiller, so I could join the upperclassmen's weight training group. My strength shot up tremendously when I got to work out everyday with the older guys I wanted to impress.

I still used the original rope system my dad rigged up in middle school to lift weights. The weights were tied up with a rope around their center loophole and I'd work on a series of exercises to strengthen my upper body. The lift I became the strongest at was the butterfly press, which is my modified bench press. The motion involves me lying on my back on a flat bench-press and shooting the weights skyward.

Dan Gable often tells the story that his goal in training was to be so exhausted that he would have to be carried out of the wrestling room. He didn't feel he exhausted himself until he passed out or was at the edge of sanity. I use that same philosophy when I'm training to go beyond the limits of exhaustion and pain.

After all the heavy lifting, I was sweaty and sore for the rest of the day at school—but the weight training really paid off during my first high school wrestling season. My strength improved so much that I finally broke the ropes I was using to tie free-weights to my arms.

The ropes came close to breaking on several occasions after I started to use heavier weights, causing more wear and tear on the gear. They finally broke—of all times, right as I was arguing with my dad about using something different to hold the weights in place.

One side gave up and snapped, causing the weights to tumble down that side with nothing there to hold them. Suddenly my other arm had over 100 pounds pulling down on it with no counterbalance. The weights crashed to the ground, slingshotting me across the room! Even I had to laugh.

I used small, sturdy chains after that ordeal, which I didn't outgrow for another two years of hard weight training.

The gains I made in weight training as a freshman were some of the fastest strength gains I've ever made, because my body started to get used to working out on a regular basis. Since then I haven't gone for any extended period without a dose of intense lifting to stay in good form.

The first wrestling practice in the fall was the usual tough wake-up call. We began the practices with a lot of conditioning to make sure that everyone would be ready for the live wrestling we'd do later on.

Those first two weeks of practice we spent running indoors in sweats and outside. We did stretching with strength work to help our bodies acclimate to the rigors of practicing for months in the middle of the winter. And we did drills that strained muscles I didn't know I had.

All throughout the first week, Coach Ramos had one of the wrestling managers time me on a stopwatch and make sure I didn't stop my bearcrawl running for at least ten minutes everyday. It's demanding for a lot of people to run at a good pace for ten minutes without taking a breather, but since I was doing bearcrawls, I felt like I ran for miles.

I never liked having to condition for wrestling with anything but live wrestling action. On the other hand, in time I came to understand why Coach Ramos had us doing these drills. Every wrestler ends up slacking back into poor technique when they get tired. He wanted us to train to a level where we'd have more stamina to execute consistently and with good technique. He wasn't going to stop the conditioning regimen until he thought we were ready.

When the conditioning practices ended, Ramos divided the room in half. He put most of the juniors and seniors on the experienced side of the room to work on high level techniques. The other half of the room was left to the new and intermediate wrestlers in their first or second year.

I assumed after working with him for so long that I'd already qualify for the experienced half of the team. I felt like I knew everything there was to know. But Coach Ramos put me on the less-experienced side of the room, and I worked with other freshman wrestlers, most of whom hadn't wrestled at all before.

I was frustrated at the start of the season and shared these feelings with my parents. They brought me back down to earth. No time devoted to relearning the basics is wasted time, because the basics are essential. Once I accepted that I needed to go back and review the basics, I focused on making a spot on the team. I had my eyes set on the varsity lineup from the get go, but there were two terrific wrestlers in my weight class who were both much better than I was at the time.

My friend Sean Patrick, a freshman, ended up taking the varsity spot from another friend, junior Michael Bui. Sean was one of two freshmen who made it to the varsity lineup; the other was my friend Nick Lucaks. Nick and I had wrestled since the sixth grade. It was impressive to see that two freshman—Nick won the 112 pound varsity spot—could be as successful as they were. Their success was a huge argument in favor of the youth team that had given us our start.

I made the decision to drop a little weight and wrestle in the 95 pound weight class for the junior varsity team, which had an open spot. I was the only freshman on our JV team, which would've been competitive with most of the varsity teams in the state. The JV teams we wrestled against were still tough competition, but we never felt overmatched.

Wrestling is a sport where it's natural to develop rivalries with specific opponents. There was one tough wrestler I faced twice my freshman year. I lost both times. He wrestled for our rivals, the Parkview Panthers. I wanted to beat him so badly, but I never did. He was a very tough wrestler who wasn't afraid to get in and mix it up with me. We wrestled in the finals of two tournaments, where I took 2nd place both times.

I finished the year with a strong 2nd place finish at the JV County Championships and a 5th place finish at the King of the Hill tournament, equivalent to the JV State Championships. My rival won both tournaments.

I learned a lot that first year, mostly from observing the bouts between older wrestlers. I had a blast watching the varsity matches and envisioning the time when I'd have the chance to compete at the same level. Determined to work hard enough over the summer to come back and break the varsity lineup, I told everyone that I wouldn't be satisfied until I was the varsity 103 pound wrestler for the Collins Hill Eagles.

I focused on quite a few other things when the wrestling season ended, so my total dedication to wrestling faltered a bit. I lifted weights but didn't do too much work in the practice room until we went to the team's summer camp at Appalachian State University. It wasn't until then that I learned about an up-and-coming wrestler I would have to compete against.

Tyler Parker was my teammate and friend who started wrestling with the 8th grade wrestling team. He soared in his freshman year at Collins Hill, and in my sophomore season he became the varsity's 103 pound star, which meant I had another year to wrestle on JV.

Tyler's path was completely different from mine: he was one of the top wrestlers in the state in his first season. He wasn't the most graceful or strong looking wrestler, but he was very intelligent and deceptively solid.

Sean Patrick, who had held the varsity spot in that weight class the year before, placed 4th in the state tournament as a freshman. Nick Lucaks, the other freshman, ended up with a 4th place finish at the 112 pound weight class. As last year's varsity freshmen sensations, they made room for Tyler as they got bigger.

Tyler was way too much for me to handle. I was glad he was doing so well, but I was disappointed by the fact that I would've already broken through the varsity lineup by now had I been on a different team.

Coach Ramos was known for producing a lot of great lightweight wrestlers, because his practices were geared towards people his size. Coach Ramos isn't the most imposing man in the world (he wrestled collegiately at 118 pounds), but he's made an oversized impact as a coach.

I had another year as the JV starter, but I wasn't planning on cutting weight to get back down to 95 pounds until the team needed me to. I wrestled most of my sophomore season at the 103 pound weight class and did well against the larger opponents.

Coach Ramos realized the JV team's potential and started lining us up against some varsity teams. We had a full lineup of fourteen wrestlers at every weight class, and there was no reason why we couldn't beat the varsity squads. We held our own against varsity teams and began to show the dominance of the Collins Hill program as a whole.

I trained hard my sophomore season with the goal of dominating the JV state championships, which were hosted by Collins Hill that year. I returned to my 95 pound weight class and was a lot stronger pound for pound than I had ever been. My friend and teammate, freshman Cody Black, moved into the 103 pound spot as I dropped down a weight class, and we offered tough competition for one another in the practice room every day. We were geared up and ready to take on any-one at the end of the season.

In my heart, I badly wanted the championship medal and the respect it symbolized. On the day of the tournament, I couldn't wait for everything to start. Our team had added a new coach, Eric Erbach, one of the best motivators I'd ever seen. He got our JV team fired up before every match.

I destroyed my first two opponents; my last match of the day was more of a challenge. He was a good wrestler, but he couldn't stop me from barreling into his legs to secure takedown after takedown. So I was three for three at the end of day one.

I made weight for the final time in the season that Friday night, and then went home to wait for the semi-finals on Saturday morning.

The school was close enough to my house that I could drive my wheelchair up to the gym. On Saturday, I decided to ride up by myself, blaring rock music and getting a little bit of fresh air before I was stuck inside of the tournament all day.

I met a girl on the second day of King of the Hill named Hannah. She was a wrestling manager for another team and her brother was one of the 189 pound wrestlers competing. Talking to her kept me relaxed and fresh.

I knew I still had to keep my focus and that I wouldn't be beat-ing anyone if I didn't have a sharp mental edge. But like any other red-blooded American male, this girl just made me a little more intense. I breezed through the semi-finals in the morning and as I waited for the finals, I talked with Hannah. When my match came, I was too intense for my own good.

I had beaten this wrestler before. He was from Starr's Mill High School. And I was confident—here I was in the finals, surrounded by family and friends, and I wasn't the underdog. So I decided to put on a show and try to impress Hannah—and I almost got disqualified for doing it.

I used moves that I didn't need to, keeping so much pressure on the other wrestler that he tripped and fell on his face. He jumped in the air to keep me from catching him, but I brought him down anyway. The wrestler was a good guy who I was already friends with and got to know better down the road, but on that day, I went overboard to beat him.

The intensity of my match got my teammate Cody Black fired up to finish off his opponent with a pin for 3rd place at the 103 pound class. The domino effect from our energy shot through the rest of our lineup. We won in almost every weight class in which we had a finals competitor.

It was quite an honor to stand on top of the podium and have the medal placed around my neck. But with that goal accomplished, I set my next one on achieving the same victory at the varsity level.

Coach Ramos and the rest of the coaches on the team understood how challenging it was to break the varsity lineup, so they offered other opportunities for their wrestlers to receive varsity letters. I lettered at the end of my sophomore season for having two seasons under my belt as a JV wrestler. It motivated me even more heavily to break the lineup.

Tyler Parker—who was my training partner—won his first state championship as a freshman at the 103 pound weight class. Though it was especially hard to make varsity at Collins Hill because of our depth of talent, I knew that hard training with Tyler would pay off. I also made the extra effort to attend camps and step up my training regimen so I could improve various aspects of my wrestling over the summer.

I made vast improvements in both strength and technique from the end of my sophomore season to the beginning of my junior year. I was prepared for anyone.

But I wasn't just a wrestler. I was student, and a teenager. I got a lot more actively involved in other programs at school. I was getting good grades in school and taking all honors and AP classes. I started going to my church's youth group every Wednesday and going to meetings of the Fellowship of Christian Athletes at school once a week. I had a lot of friends at Collins Hill, and I was elected one of the junior class representatives for the homecoming court, along with my good friends Chip Daymude, Peyton Dennard, and Britanny Patterson. As we walked down the center of the football field together at our homecoming game, I couldn't believe that my peers had reached this point of accepting me as one of their own.

Everything in my life appeared to be falling into place. Then the wrestling season came—and with it, the wrestle-off to determine the varsity and junior varsity lineups.

The result was rough. Thomas Knapp, a freshman who started wrestling before I had, went to the 103 pound weight class. He was an extremely tough wrestler, but a good friend outside of competition. Cody Black, a good friend and my best practice partner, ended up at the 112 pound slot on varsity after putting on a lot of muscle over the summer.

So I spent a lot of time traveling with the varsity team and going to the matches as the back-up. But I had a good number of varsity matches myself in my junior year, earning me a win-loss record of 11-2. I faced a lot of the lower end competition that Coach Ramos didn't want Thomas injuring himself against, but I also faced off against a couple of very tough wrestlers. I beat two state-qualifiers that year, which was a huge accomplishment because it instilled the confidence I needed to come back for my senior season and lay claim to the 103 pound weight class.

I concentrated a lot more on schoolwork, because I knew that my wrestling career would be over in a matter of years, and that I needed a good education to carry me beyond that. I took two AP classes in Spanish and Statistics to get some college credit before I jumped into a university. Judson Bridges, my Spanish teacher, was a terrific influence on me and was nominated for the Georgia Teacher of the Year Award.

The most fun I had all year was at the end of the season when I entered the "Mr. Collins Hill" contest, which was the school's amateur bodybuilding show. It packed the theater every year with hundreds of screaming girls.

Some people got intense about the competition and worked real hard to sculpt their bodies and cut down like any bodybuilder would. I did the competition for fun and had a great time doing it. I did go to a tanning bed for about a month before the competition to make sure I looked good on the school's theater stage, and I tried to show up the other ripped guys on stage by doing a handstand push-up in the free pose. The event was a fundraising opportunity for the football team, but we all took it as a time to show off in front of the whole school. The school's news channel taped the competition and played it the next day.

Far more serious than Mr. Collins Hill was the task of getting ready for my senior season on the wrestling mat. I drilled at wrestling camps all summer long after my junior year. Now I was a senior in high school, and it was my last time to make an impact, break the varsity lineup, and win a state championship. I kept up with my weight-training, did my bear crawl sprints, and did shadow wrestling whenever I couldn't find an opponent.

I had to cut a lot more weight to get down to the 103 pound weight class my senior season. My teachers were very understanding. It's not easy to sit in class with your stomach growling while a teacher lobbies for your attention. They knew I was listening, however disoriented I might seem, daydreaming about food that I couldn't eat. And I kept working out relentlessly.

I realized that I'd rather work out alone because I could push myself harder when there wasn't anyone around to distract me. Sometimes I caught myself grimacing or struggling with a weight just for the added impact it had on people watching. When I didn't have to impress anyone, I was the only one responsible for how intensely I practiced, and I didn't have a reason to be self-conscious or give in to the temptation to put on a show for others. I could concentrate on the weights and on the work.

I focused on the important mental aspects of the sport. When I was tired, I knew that my mind was trying to convince my muscles that they couldn't move anymore. But I knew deep down that they could and that it was only a mental limit that was holding me back. When I finally broke down that limiting barrier in my mind, I realized how much further I could actually go.

Coach Ramos came by one day and saw me in the wrestling room doing my own thing—shadow wrestling and running. He told me that I was going to be a great wrestler this year, and I needed to work that hard all season long if I expected to hold onto it. I told him that I could feel the hourglass pouring away. I was committed to making the most out of my senior year.

I was ready for the season to start. It was time to take what was rightfully mine from the beginning: my varsity spot.

There are few things as powerful as having people in your life who want to see you succeed and thrive. Most goodhearted people are willing to help others and make sacrifices - they only ask that other people do the same. And finding people like that in your own life begins with serving others.

CHAPTER 10 **Heroes**

have been blessed with many role models in my life. I've never looked at myself as a role model, but I do believe in trying my best to make a difference in people's lives. And I've met and known many people who've had a profound influence on mine.

In many ways, I'm just a normal nineteen-year-old male. I haven't had any formal training in psychology or quantum physics. I observe things I see and feel through emotion and interpret them accordingly. God has given me whatever insight and intuition I have to offer, mixed in with a lot of trial and error.

I've taken the things I've learned through facing challenges in my life and tried to pass them on to others. I'm surprised and pleased that so many people have told me how my example has been a motivation to them.

Because I am blessed with a great family, I've never needed to look very far to find my role models. They've taught me about life, love, and compassion. And they've taught me about faith and Jesus Christ, which is the most important aspect of my life. I may be one of those few people who hope it's true that we all turn into our parents when we grow older.

My mother is the one who always motivated me to reach out to others, to offer them the support that she's always offered me. And I know she will never back down when there's something her kids want that's within her reach.

My father is a teacher, a motivator, an athlete, and a fixer, always teaching me that I could do anything and solve any problem. And my dad is tough. He always told me to avoid bullies and never start a fight, but that if I was ever in one, I should finish it.

Most people tell me they know how incredible my parents must be, without ever having met them. I think this is because my parents raised me not as being abnormal, but simply as their child. They instilled certain values and ideas in all of their children, regardless of physical capability. They taught us to never quit, to give our all in every way, and that if we got a C grade, we wouldn't have a house to come home to. They challenged us, but they also trusted us, and they were never *too* strict.

I know my parents were put in a difficult situation at a young age. But they held things together through their love for each other and for their children. I know they've been role models for parents of disabled children around the country. My parents taught me never to hate my physical limits. When the doctors discussed cutting off my feet so it would be easier for me to wear prosthetics, my parents said no—I wasn't going to pretend to be different. I was their child, and that's what mattered most.

My sisters have always been great, too. Even if it would be easy for them to just be annoyed that I'm not like other brothers, I've listened to them stick up for disabled kids when others mock or make fun of them, and I'm proud of their compassion. They're terrific athletes, beautiful girls, and hard working students. I'm a little rough on them when it comes to their boyfriends, but deep down I know they appreciate having an overprotective big brother. I have no doubt they'll go on to accomplish whatever they desire.

I have a lot of love for my dad's parents. When my father took me to every one of my wrestling matches, he was following in the footsteps of my Grandpa Hobert, who did the same for him. As for my Grandma Carla, she's a fun lady, a hairdresser, and the type of grandma who will hook me up with a date on the beach during vacation.

Grandma Betty, on my mother's side, has showed me a lot of love and support since I was an infant. She's had a big influence on my life and is always there with my Grandpa Norm for every family sporting event. She's done everything from helping me draft my first speech to teaching me how to make peanut brittle at Christmas.

My Grandpa Norm is my biggest role model. He's the kindest man I've ever known. I've only seen him upset one time in my life, which happened to be because as a six year old I tried to hide in the huge pool of balls at a Chuck E. Cheese, not wanting to leave. He was an athlete in high school, served in the Air Force, and was a valedictorian engineering graduate from the University of Illinois.

He used to run marathons and did well until he suffered a major heart attack shortly after we moved to Georgia. My grandpa toughed out quadruple bypass surgery immediately following the heart attack and still exercises at the age of 72. I used to joke with him when I was younger that he was getting old with his gray hair, but all of my grandparents are still young and vibrant on the inside.

More importantly, Grandpa Norm is a true man of God. He sat with me at Sunday school until I was able to handle myself, because he wanted me to be able to learn about Jesus. For years, he's been a Sunday school teacher himself. He is a model for those who seek to live as Christ-like leaders in their community.

One very big source of motivation for me has been my cousin, Hollie. She has the sweetest heart of anyone I've ever met, but has more obstacles to contend with than even I can know.

She was born in Virginia three years after me, the firstborn daughter to my mom's older brother. As a newborn, she suffered massive seizures. It took the doctors several days to diagnose the problem, but by then it was already too late: the seizures had damaged her brain. They happened because Hollie was born without the ability to process the ammonia in her bloodstream.

The doctors didn't expect Hollie to live more than a year—but she's 16 years old now and the oldest living person ever with her disorder. Hollie refuses to give up on life time and time again. She has to visit her local hospital in Indiana frequently, but she has not stopped fighting through every obstacle.

I love my cousin very much, even though ignorant people might single her out as slow or different from other people. Hollie will have to live the rest of her life without the ability to communicate, except for a little sign-language. But even though Hollie can't communicate like everyone else, she offers more love to those around her than anyone I've ever seen. And Hollie has a family that will never give up on her.

Outside of my family, I've always thrived on the friendship and support of others. My high school wrestling coach, Cliff Ramos, has influenced me more than anyone I've ever known. He chose to make wrestlers out of inexperienced athletes and men out of boys.

Coach Ramos has stood alongside and guided me through the most challenging times of my life, helping me to achieve my dreams. He has always been there to teach and motivate me, and he's understood me, he knows what I'm trying to do and how best to get me there.

When someone accepts responsibility as a coach, they take on a huge task. Coaches have to walk the fine line as friends, teachers, disciplinarians, and mentors. Coaches must gain their athletes' trust before asking them to perform at their peak levels. And once that trust is achieved, the bond between a coach and an athlete never breaks.

Even though I've graduated and moved onto the University of Georgia's collegiate wrestling, he is still one of the most influential people in my life. Coach Ramos worked with me for many years, teaching me how to wrestle, nurturing me when I knew nothing about the sport, and working to address my physical and mental needs. By the time I left, I wanted to wrestle for Coach Ramos more than I did for Collins Hill.

Coach Ramos would always restrain his enthusiasm after a match regardless of the outcome. But my teammates and I knew when we had made him proud, and when we let him down. When we lost matches we should've won, Coach Ramos would communicate his disappointment without ever speaking a word.

The bond between coach and student was deeper in my case, because I was a unique challenge to Coach Ramos. Facing that unique challenge built a special relationship between us. When the team traveled, Coach Ramos and I would room together with my drill partner and friend, Cody Black. It wasn't because I needed the extra help, but because we all enjoyed the time spent with one another. He constantly joked about having to tolerate my heavy snoring, which *is* actually pretty bad, when we shared a room on trips.

One night, on a trip to a wrestling tournament in North Carolina, Cody and I woke up to find several parents banging on our hotel room door. The parents took Coach Ramos into the bathroom, closing the door behind them.

It turned out that Coach Ramos' son Trevor, who was a former wrestler for Collins Hill, had been a passenger in a severe car accident. The driver had been drinking, crashed the vehicle into a tree, and fled the scene, leaving Trevor unconscious in the passenger seat.

The car caught fire, and two high schoolers tried to pull Trevor out of the burning car. They got him out and to the hospital, but he had already suffered massive brain trauma from the collision.

Coach Ramos looked like a different person when we saw him sitting in the bathroom, waiting for a friend to drive him to the hospital. Cody and I still remember the look on his face. We couldn't believe what had happened, but we sat on the bed and prayed for the father and son.

We still had to wrestle in the tournament the next day, but it was a difficult challenge without Coach Ramos in our corner. In the end, Trevor made a tremendous recovery. He was the kicker for the University of West Georgia, and he ultimately came back to play his last year in college—even after doctors doubted whether or not he'd survive his injuries from the crash. But miracles happen—and Trevor experienced a miracle.

For me, meeting Coach Ramos was a miracle, or rather, a godsend. He changed my life immeasurably for the better. And he was a motivator who kept me pushing hard against any perceived limits.

The daily grind of a wrestling exercise program leaves anyone exhausted, but Coach knew what I was capable of doing, and he made me break through barriers that seemed insurmountable.

Coach Ramos is a man of integrity. He never forced people to cut weight. He never asked them to do anything that would risk their health. He encouraged good sportsmanship, and he taught us to never make excuses. His wrestlers go to study hall to keep their grades up and aren't allowed to wrestle if they fail more than one class. He even makes the wrestlers do extra work (like running stadium stairs) for C's and D's in classes he knows they can do better in.

Even with my special challenges, Coach Ramos treated me like any other wrestler on his team, which was exactly how I wanted to be treated. If he had treated me as if I were disabled or feeble, I would've never beaten a single opponent. Coach Ramos wasn't there to wipe the crumbs off my lap every time I ate a meal. He was there to make me the best wrestler I could be.

Coach Ramos made me earn my own way and fight for my position on the team. No one gave me my spot as a varsity wrestler: I had to earn it. But Coach Ramos saw that I could do it and trained me to carry my own weight as a valuable member of the team.

I will never forget when our varsity team traveled to Cleveland, Tennessee during my senior season, for a wrestling tournament. The matches continued all day long, and we wrestled some of the toughest teams from the South.

Coach Ramos saw that a lot of our wrestlers weren't performing as well as they should have been. He was especially upset with the ones who were complaining about injuries in order to duck out of the rest of the tournament competition.

I wrestled my toughest match of the day in the semi-finals of the tournament. I had won the previous two matches by pins, but I knew I'd be in for a war in the last one. The kid I was facing was one of the top-ranking wrestlers in Tennessee in my weight class.

Our match was brutal. The opposing team had wrestling cheerleaders, and we even occasionally scrambled off the mat, crashed into the girls, and kept fighting.

The match ended up going all the way to double-overtime. I lost the match in the last ten seconds as my opponent scored an escape to defeat me, but I had fought as hard as I could.

Coach Ramos could see that I was in a lot of discomfort, but I wouldn't tell him what the problem was until after I cooled off from the defeat. I told him that in the midst of fighting to defend one of the takedowns, I had painfully stretched my groin. Earlier in the day, I had battered one of my shoulders against an opponent's body, and it had gotten progressively worse through every match.

He brought the team together for a meeting after the semi-final matches, before the last matches began. I had never seen him so upset over the performance of the team, but he was most upset by the fact that a few of my teammates didn't seem to care about the outcome of the match.

He told us to start cheering for our teammates and not sit back complaining. He then singled me out by saying that I was one of the only wrestlers on the team who had the right to make an excuse or complain about an injury, and I wasn't complaining or moaning or asking to be excused. He said I was one of the only wrestlers who cared more about winning or losing than about being injured. It was a speech that made everyone snap to attention for the finals.

Coach Ramos cared about helping his wrestlers grow academically, morally, and physically. Nothing was as important to him as his family and his wrestlers. I believe they go hand-in-hand with him, which is what makes him so remarkable.

Coach Ramos gave generously of his knowledge and understanding. He allowed me to think independently, and taught me how to use my God-given abilities. He taught me to take risks, because you can't grow as a person if you don't.

Someday, I want to have the same impact that he has on the kids that he coaches with a team of my own. He is the embodiment of a great role model and mentor.

I also have many other role models who've influenced me in more general ways, whether I've known them closely or not.

True role models are self-sacrificing. They are ready and willing to do what's right for the sake of humanity, at any cost. True role models don't expect to be thanked at the end of the day for what they do. They just do what's right.

That's why my personal role models are the men and women fighting in the Armed Forces. These brave souls sacrifice their own lives without hesitation to help bring freedom to people who had no hope in the Middle East.

I'm inspired that the soldiers serving the United States are protecting my rights as a citizen of this wonderful country. Since I was four years old, I've looked at soldiers as heroes. I used to ask my father about his time in the military and imagine myself in the same setting. He'd chant march songs about the Airborne Rangers, and I was desperate to become one.

I've always wanted to serve in the military. I held onto that dream until I was in high school. I took the Armed Services Aptitude and Battery (ASVAB) exam that all people in the military take. I scored well on every part of the exam (except for the mechanic sections), and I hoped I had done well enough to land a position with Army Intelligence or my dream job, the Airborne Rangers.

I spoke with a couple of recruiters, and one in particular was receptive, but she told me that the only way I'd be able to serve was as a chaplain. My immediate response was to ask: Do they get rifle trained too? She informed me that they do not, but that they do have a personal assistant. That didn't flow along the same lines as what I had in mind when I went to take the exam, but I did give it some thought.

Rangers train very similarly to wrestlers. They're up early in the morning, running all day, and train for a special kind of combat. I feel as though I'd already be accustomed to the intensity of the lifestyle, and I wish I was able to serve as they do.

Good soldiers don't question orders from their commanding officers, just as good wrestlers don't question the judgment of a good coach. Soldiers work hard in preparation to win battles and contribute their piece to a campaign, the same as wrestlers work to win their individual matches and contribute to the success of the team.

Soldiers, firemen, police officers, ambulance drivers, and the Homeland Security staff all do their duty, frequently in thankless positions, to ensure the safety of every American. They are true role models because they are willing to sacrifice their lives for the freedoms we enjoy.

Some of these same people, whether it is through the attacks of war or the danger of their positions, end up losing part or all of their limbs. It's a sad part of the job they do.

I've met some of these individuals, people who've gone through their whole lives without having to adapt to not having the use of all their limbs. Now they're faced with many of the same challenges I've dealt with in my own life, along with the added feeling of the physical loss of the abilities they had from birth—something I can only begin to imagine.

I want to have as much of an impact on these brave individuals as I can, if to only show them that their dreams are not lost because of their condition. These heroes can continue to lead full lives, and they can also have a powerful impact on people. They serve as a constant reminder that we wouldn't have the most basic things we value in our everyday lives—peace, freedom, and security—if they didn't sacrifice their bodies and themselves on our behalf.

Our men and women in uniform are all so young, most just a few years older than I am. They are too young to lose their limbs. They are too young to die. But if they do, it will be in place of you and me. It will be for a cause greater than themselves.

I believe America is the greatest nation in the world, in part because we have such strong role models to look up to—whether they are kind teachers, motivating coaches, caring parents, or brave soldiers serving in the line of duty. We are blessed to have them in our lives, and we should honor their sacrifice.

Regardless of what your dreams may be, you alone know the extent you've sacrificed. If you are able to look in the mirror and see that you have gone beyond your own limits - the limits of exhaustion, of dedication, of fear - to get the job done and achieve the goal, then you're on the right track. If you want something bad enough, you're going to fight hard for it.

CHAPTER II **One Last Season**

I *was overweight before my senior season began*. I had trouble getting down to 103 pounds for summer camp, and I needed to stay there until after nationals in April. Three years was a long time to be in such a low weight class. Most seniors move up in weight, but this was the weight class in which I felt most competitive.

My exercise regimen remained intense all year, but I did change the way I lifted during the season, to some degree. In the off-season, I looked to make large strength gains. So I'd eat a lot more and lift heavier weight to gain bulk. The bulk gave me raw power and a greater ability to train, since body size has a direct correlation to the amount of weight a person can handle.

In the middle of the season, my workouts consisted mostly of light repetitions for three main reasons. The first reason was that heavier weight carries a higher risk of injuring me. So I lifted lighter weight more times to avoid tearing out my shoulders. Second, light repetitions trained my body to build lasting bursts of strength. Instead of a one-shot maximum lift, the repetitions took me longer, training my body to exert force for a period of minutes—like a wrestling match. Finally, lifting heavier weights usually causes people to gain body weight, and my goal was to stay as close to 103 pounds as possible.

As the wrestling season approached, I was training almost entirely for repetitions and I was feeling giant power gains every week. My drill partner, Cody Black, commented on how much stronger I felt than the year before. Cody was a state qualifier from the previous year and we'd wrestled more matches together in practice than just about anyone else on the team. He worked hard in the weight room too, which gave us big strength advantages over our opponents at 103 and 112 pounds.

My teammates helped me set up my weights when I trained. They'd gather the free weights that I asked for and loop my chains through the holes in the center. Then I'd lie back on a bench press and they'd slide the arm bands that the chains were attached to onto my arms.

I'd work hard in my weight training class and do shorter workouts after school. My workouts were never too long, probably because we only had about 50 minutes in the weight room after we got dressed out. I had weight training as my second to last class of the day senior year, which meant I had to go to statistics class right afterwards.

Every so often, we'd have a quiz or test in statistics after I went through an intense chest exercise. I sometimes struggled to bring my arms together to hold a pencil because I'd be shaking so badly after the workout.

I had the opportunity to do more with my lifting than just work out, however. I was contacted by professional bodybuilder and GNC Personal Trainer Dave Hawk about a chance to lift in a large fitness expo, the Show of Strength, hosted by the city of Atlanta. Dave told me he was partnering with bodybuilding legend Lee Haney to put on a teen competition with the surrounding high schools. Dave wanted me to participate on the show's main stage and work with GNC and Maximum Human Performance (MHP) to help me showcase a personal display of strength.

After we did research into record-breaking lifts, Dave informed me that I'd be recognized as the unofficial World's Strongest Teen if I could butterfly press 200 pounds more than 15 times. The weight itself was nearly twice my bodyweight, but I figured I'd train for it and see what happened.

I spent the next month and a half working on rep after rep with the weight he wanted me to lift. It was a hard undertaking, and the training wore me out, but I could feel the excitement around the people who helped me lift every day.

Because the record was a comparison between the weight lifted, number of reps, and my bodyweight at the time of the lift, I had to get down to my wrestling weight of 103 pounds to get the record. It was tough to lose weight and make strength gains at the same time. I cut carbohydrates almost entirely out of my diet as the competition crept up.

The day finally came. My friends and family were there in downtown Atlanta when I contended for the GNC Show of Strength world record. I was fired up and ready to go when my time came to step on stage and wrap the bands around my arms. I could feel my heart racing and I hoped the extra adrenaline would pump out a few more reps.

I felt great during the warm-up and decided to lift with 120 pounds on each arm—a total of 240 pounds, well over twice my body weight. The free weights felt awfully heavy hanging down on the chains as my dad slipped them securely on me. They clanged against one another when I pulled them close to my body for the first repetition.

I took a deep breath and felt my heart pump one last time before I exhaled all of the air in my lungs in an effort to launch the weights up. I heard the announcer counting in what seemed like a faraway voice: "One . . . two . . . three . . ."

The crowd picked up on the rhythm and I kept pushing the reps out with slightly more effort each time. I could feel the fatigue starting to set in after I hit the 12th rep and the burn began when I got past number 17. I didn't stop and I knew I could go on for a while longer when I hit 20, but not by much.

I told myself I could handle 5 more reps at most, but I thought 25 was too boring a number, so I scaled it back by 2 and dropped the plates on the floor after my 23rd repetition. The last thing to go through my mind before I dropped the plates was that Michael Jordan wore number 23—and somehow, that made the number seem much cooler.

I had broken the world record. I finished the lift with 23 repetitions of 240 pounds, which qualified as 2.33 times my bodyweight. It was an unbelievable experience to set the record and reach my personal peak at weightlifting, but I had a long and demanding wrestling season ahead that would define what I was really made of.

The wrestling tournament schedule had one of the toughest competitions in the southeast at the very beginning of the season. My team was traveling to Winston Salem, North Carolina, to wrestle the top competitors from nearby states.

My Collins Hill teammates and I wrestled off for spots in the varsity lineup before we left for the tournament and there wasn't anyone to even challenge me for my spot. I was too strong, experienced, and dominant by now. I did miss the competition of battling my own teammates in the practice room, but I knew I deserved my varsity spot regardless. It was everything I had worked so hard for.

As this was a pre-season match, I didn't feel too much pressure. My bigger concern was about cutting down to 103 pounds for the first time since summer wrestling camp where I had a record of 10 wins and 1 loss.

I had a tough bracket in Winston Salem and ended up with a sixth place finish. I wasn't disappointed with the placement, but I was upset about one match. It was in the tournament's quarterfinals, which paired me against a challenging opponent from Florida. I ended up losing the match because the kid refused to wrestle me; he scored three points and ran away the rest of the match.

My opponent locked up really tight with me in the first period, where we struggled back and forth, but neither one of us scored. In the second period of the match, he escaped from bottom, causing me to fall behind 1-0. He scored a takedown from pushing my head down and spinning around behind me to make the score 3-0. I started to come back with an escape to make the match 3-1, but he was comfortable enough with his 2 point lead that he decided not to wrestle anymore.

He stayed as far away from me as possible, especially when we were close to the center of the mat. He was slightly more aggressive on the boundaries because he could run out of bounds if he got in any danger.

My only hope was to fatigue the kid as much as I could, so I continued to keep the pressure on him as best I could. The match seemed to drag on for an eternity before the second period came to a close.

My opponent was exhausted at this point, and I could feel it. When the third period started he hardly had enough energy to run away anymore. He called for an injury timeout, claiming that he hurt his ankle. It only infuriated me more when I came to the conclusion that he was wasting time to catch his breath.

He called for a second injury timeout right afterwards, but the referee never penalized him—even though that's what the rules require. Coach Ramos was incensed that the referee ignored my opponent's stalling, so he told me to try out the 'rope-a-dope' move that we worked on in practice for a situation exactly like this one.

The other wrestler ran with his back to me when the match started again. I tried one last time to chase him around the wrestling mat but couldn't get close enough to score. For all the advantage I have in strength, I don't have the speed to catch someone in a situation like that. So I tried the 'rope-a-dope' move for the first time in a match.

The move called for me to lie on my back with one shoulder down in the middle of the mat. It was supposed to entice him to come close enough for me to grab hold of him because he'd be tempted to get the quick pin or score points off an easy takedown. He started to inch in closer when I dropped down to my back, but his coach yelled at him to move away.

The referee actually warned me for unsportsmanlike conduct because he claimed I was taunting the other wrestler by lying on my back. That would be understandable under normal circumstances but I was doing everything in my power to bring this wrestler in close enough to actually wrestle. I wasn't taunting, I was trying to get to grips with him and score a takedown.

I was told that I couldn't use the 'rope-a-dope' in the match again without being penalized for it, so I continued to run after the kid. I couldn't get close enough to lock up, and the referee waited until the end of the match to make a stalling call against my opponent.

A referee can call a stalling penalty at his discretion, whenever he thinks a wrestler is not taking any kind of action to actually wrestle. Some referees would have disqualified my opponent for running away. Most would have penalized him points to force him back into action.

The match ended with a score of 3-2 after I received one point for my opponent's blatant stalling. It was so obvious that a lot of other wrestlers came over and told me how wrong they thought my opponent's tactics had been, and how remiss the referee had been to not penalize him earlier and force the action.

Still, I used the tournament loss as a motivator as we swung into local competition in Georgia the next weekend, the first competition of the regular season. We faced a total of five teams at a tournament in Central Gwinnett High School's gym, but the teams were nowhere near the level of those from North Carolina.

I pinned my way through each of the matches that weekend, and most wrestlers from Collins Hill began with an undefeated regular season record. Coach Ramos didn't like us wrestling below our full potential, but it was important to have a couple of matches where we could warm-up against teams we had no problem with.

We wrestled our home opener on Wednesday of the next week against Pope High School. It was a big adrenaline rush to be announced as a varsity starter in front of 500 parents, students, and teachers who came to see the match.

The match itself was quite a show. The gym had every light turned out but the spotlight that dropped down from the ceiling to shine on the center of the mat, illuminating the two wrestlers. Each wrestler was announced and a few seconds of their intro theme song was played to fire everyone up.

There was a total of fourteen of us wearing matching green and white warm-up suits, and we drilled as a team to get ready under the spotlight with Linkin Park's music blaring and the hometown fans cheering. I came out to my theme song, Chevelle's "Send the Pain Below." To be honest, when my match came, I had so much adrenaline flowing that I hardly remember the match except that I won easily, by points, scoring takedowns at will.

The following weekend's tournament was almost as incredible. It was our second regular season tournament, and our lineup was almost entirely full now that the football season had ended and the two-sport wrestlers had joined our team.

The Walton Duals tournament format was what is called a 'Dual-Meet Tournament,' where multiple teams are formed in a bracket, and two teams wrestle one another to see who scores more overall team points. The winning team advances to the next round, and no wrestlers from that team are eliminated, as they might be in an individual tournament. Team points are scored by pins for 6 points, technical falls or mercy-rule victories for 5 points, major decisions that yield 4 team points, and minor decisions that yield 3 team points.

The Walton Duals hosted eight high schools from Georgia and Tennessee. We wrestled Pope High School in our first match in a rematch from three days earlier. I had a closer match and won by a minor decision, but the rest of the team breezed through without an issue.

Our toughest match faced us next: the semi-finals against the McEachern Indians, our rivals from the neighboring county. They wrestled hard-fought matches against every one of our guys and I lost my first match of the regular season in an exhilarating bout with a score of 12-11.

The team score went on to be tied up at 32 to 32 at the end of all the matches. The coaches and referee convened and finally decided that Collins Hill has won the match because we had one more pin than our cross-county rivals.

Our schedule usually had a dual meet match during the week and tournaments on the weekends. For my senior season, we started practice in October and went on until the beginning of April for the nationals. I was getting accustomed to wrestling on the varsity squad, and I slowly got used to keeping my weight down during the week and having to shed a few extra pounds for tournament weigh-ins on the weekends.

It wasn't easy keeping my weight under control for that length of time. But the only time I had any real trouble was when I dropped down too low—staying right at 103 pounds by not eating much at all, rather than shedding pounds just before the weigh-in. I lost a lot of strength, and it drastically affected my wrestling.

There were two tournament competitions in a row which should have been easy for me, but I didn't even place because my weight was too low and I was too weak because of it. I didn't want to cut the weight if I didn't have to. Controlling my weight wasn't an issue if I was a little less than 110 pounds after practice. I could always cut seven pounds before a competition, but that's why I came in stronger.

After wrestling so poorly in those two tournaments, I made a decision to bulk up in the middle of the year. Normally this would seem like the exact opposite of what I should do, but I had to get my strength back to compete. I ate more and lifted heavier weights.

I'd start every morning by eating a small bowl of oatmeal with skim milk. For lunch, I would eat a few pieces of lunchmeat with fat free cheese, and a protein bar. Dinner was the hardest meal to keep light because I usually snacked on whatever my mom made, which was mostly salad, chicken, and a protein shake.

In no time, I saw that this method was a significantly better way for me to stay in my weight class than to just not eat at all. I ran more to burn off the extra calories, and that also helped my cardiovascular condition.

I set my eyes on the state championship from the first day of my senior season. Our practices usually lasted two and a half hours, but I'd sometimes stay for an additional two or three hours after that. I completely dedicated myself. I didn't fear any opponent I wrestled. I was committed to being a champion varsity wrestler—one who refused to give up on any match without a fight.

I eliminated distractions. I stopped watching T.V. and playing video games. I came home from practice, did my homework, listened to music, and went to bed.

I developed the mentality of a state champion. I beat a state champ from Alabama and state placers from various other states. It felt like there was no one who could stop me when I was focused. My seven-year career in the sport was peaking at the right time.

I was breezing through my competition until I suffered what should have been a season ending injury. With only three weeks left before the state tournament, my nose was shattered—broken in a grueling match at the state's largest dual-team tournament.

It happened in our team's second match of the tournament. I was facing a strong senior from Lee County High School in southern

Georgia, and in the second period, I came barreling into my opponent's body at the same time his forearm closed in around my head. He stopped my assault by dropping his arm. It wasn't intentional, but his arm crashed into my nose.

I can still remember the crunching sound of my cartilage. I felt the initial pain and backed away, trying to shake it off. We kept wrestling, and I disregarded the pain until we rolled out of bounds and the match stopped for a second. I tasted the blood trickle down the back of my throat. That was the first time I knew that something was very wrong.

I felt dazed for a while, and as we wrestled, I felt winded and disoriented, as if I couldn't get enough air in my lungs. But I refocused and finished the match strong. I lost the match with a close score. I sat against the gym's wall wondering what went wrong. I could feel the top of my nose throbbing harder and harder after the match.

The tournament was split up between Friday and Saturday, which gave me some time to go home and rest before the next match. On the way home, I mentioned what had happened and how my nose felt to my dad, but it was only slightly swollen. After we got home, my mother looked at my nose but couldn't see anything, so both of my parents made the assumption that it wasn't too bad. They probably thought I was making an excuse for losing the match, but I felt like something wasn't right with the way the pain kept pulsing.

I took an Aleve and went to sleep. I could hardly see when I woke up in the morning. My nose had swollen so much that it blocked most of my vision. I looked in the mirror and couldn't believe it. My nose was discolored and twice the size it normally was and I had a full day of wrestling ahead.

My father drove me back to the tournament for the second day's matches, and I wondered what effect my nose would have on the remaining three weeks of the season. If it was broken, it would probably have to be set and given time to heal. But time was something I didn't have. This was my one and only chance to finish my high school career as a varsity state champion.

My dad told me that, in his senior season, he had wrestled and beaten every regional state champion in Michigan. He broke his nose a few times, but the worst was in the final regional qualifying match for the state tournament. Because of the pain of the injury, he didn't even qualify for the state tournament that he almost certainly would have won.

I wasn't going to experience the same fate, no matter what. I was going to state. And it wasn't just for me. My team's aspirations for winning a championship could be shot down if I wasn't able to step back on the mat. I wasn't going to have a JV wrestler jump in, sacrificing my last chance to become a state champ and putting our team's championship level season at risk.

I talked to our team trainer and told her not to tell Coach Ramos that I was hurt, but asked her if there was anything she could do. She went to her kit and brought out the infamous sports mask that wrestlers wear when a bone in their face is broken.

I put the mask on and tried to wrestle around with a teammate in the back locker room, but while other wrestlers could adapt to the mask, I could hardly see with the thing on. Every wrestler I face is over three feet taller than I am, and the mask made it nearly impossible for me to look up at anything.

I decided not to wear the mask, and I didn't talk to Coach Ramos about the injury; and despite the swelling, he didn't ask me about it. I guess he thought if it really hurt, I would've told him. We were both trying to protect each other. In my case, I knew there was nothing he could do about my nose, so I didn't want to bother him in the midst of the semi-finals. We had to face Pope High School for the third time that season, and I had to do my part for the team.

On the mat, I pulled out a last second takedown to win my first match of the day. At the end of the bout, my face felt like someone had taken a hammer to it, and I still had another match to go.

Our last match of the day was against the toughest rival in our region: The Parkview Panthers. Their team was expected to win the state tournament, but we were fighting with everything we had to stay in contention and take the title for ourselves.

The dual meet finals were quite a production, with dimmed lights and music to start the matches. The meeting was highly anticipated. Our two teams were the best in the state and among the best in the southeast. I had faced Parkview wrestlers since sixth grade and I desperately wanted to prove to myself that I was capable of wrestling well in a big varsity finals match.

I had never been as nervous as I was heading into the final bout. I was afraid the referees would disqualify me from wrestling in the upcoming region and state tournaments because my nose looked so badly injured.

I went out and wrestled with everything I had left in me. My opponent was relentless in attacking the obvious target: my broken nose. We went to war on one another by inflicting serious pain back and forth. He attacked with a series of cross-face blows on top of my broken nose, and I locked my arms with a jawbreaker to exact some pain of my own.

It seemed like there was little I could do to stop the onslaught of points my opponent racked up. I had beaten the same wrestler by a score of 8-2 in the summer before the regular season started, but this time my opponent won the match and the Panthers dominated us in the finals of the tournament.

We took home a 2nd place finish. Coach Ramos wasn't satisfied with that, and neither were we. He used the loss to inspire us to prepare for the two important tournaments coming up.

I had one week of practice left to prepare for the regional tournament. I needed a placement in the top four to even qualify for the state tournament. I was determined to make no excuses about my broken nose. Instead, I worked harder than I ever had before.

I wouldn't leave the wrestling room until I was so fatigued from sprints and shadow wrestling that I felt like throwing up or passing out. I wanted to work so hard that it would be impossible for me to pick myself up and jump into my wheelchair to ride home. I had never put my body through such strenuous physical tests as I had in preparation for the last two weeks of the season.

The broken nose was a setback, but it would not be the end of me. It just made me evaluate where I was, where I wanted to be, and how I would get there. I knew it was a sign for me that I needed to work even harder than I had before. No matter what, I could not look back to the end of the season and feel any disappointment about the outcome. I had to work as hard as I could in the time that I was given to know that I did everything possible to secure the ultimate outcome in the end. One injury would not keep me from becoming a state champion, no matter how terrible it may have felt.

I wore the protective mask in practice, but I refused to wear it in any match that had serious ramifications on the future of my senior season. If I didn't qualify for state, my season was over.

Besides my nose, I was in the best condition of my life, and I was the second ranked wrestler in a bracket of twelve at the regional tournament. I was set behind my rival from Parkview, who had beaten me the weekend before. We were on separate sides of the bracket and could only meet in the finals, which was exactly what I was aiming to do. If I made it to the finals then I'd secure qualification for the state tournament with at least a 2nd place finish and a possibility to become the regional champion.

My first match at the tournament was with a wrestler from Oconee County High School. We hadn't wrestled before and he was obviously nervous about stepping onto the mat with me. I warmed up like normal and decided I should wrestle without wearing the mask even though he was aware of my broken nose.

My opponent capitalized immediately. He dove at my face and head butted my nose within the first 15 seconds of the match.

The pain was breathtaking. I was nearly unconscious and the referee stopped the match before the wrestler could take advantage of the cheap tactic.

I used about 45 seconds to regain my composure and get rid of the blood that dripped down, which was mostly in my throat because the break was so high up. And once the match began again, I took him straight to the ground and onto his back with a fast takedown. He was grimacing as I held him on his back, but I kept one of his shoulders lifted off the mat, and he knew that I wasn't going to pin him. I kept him from pinning himself because I had nearly 6 minutes to deal out a response to his crooked strategy. And I did.

In the end, I finished the match by beating the kid with the fifteen point mercy-rule, the technical fall coming with less than thirty seconds left in the third period.

After winning my semi-finals match by a score of 3-1, I was in the finals as a state qualifier and potential region champion. Even if I lost in the finals, I was in.

The match let loose a great deal of emotion from my family, teammates, and especially Coach Ramos. No one else had given me a chance to even win a match my first year and a half wrestling. Now I was a varsity state qualifier and had a shot at a championship.

My final match was my chance to settle the score against Parkview's 103 pounder who beat me a week before. I fought hard to win the match but he prevailed with the same strategy he had used before. He was able to score enough points and keep me away from his body. Eventually, he won.

Our team came in second place behind Parkview once again, but all 14 Collins Hill Eagles qualified with a top 4 placement in the regional tournament to go to state. Parkview only qualified 13 of their wrestlers, which gave us an advantage to close the distance between our two teams.

I was happy for my team, but not at all satisfied with my 2nd place finish. I was going to the state championships to win, not just place. So I continued to work hard, and Coach Ramos and I watched taped matches to analyze how I could improve after my two losses to the Parkview wrestler. There was the potential that I'd have to face my rival for the third weekend in a row at the state tournament in Macon, Georgia.

My experience has taught me that we have no idea how far we can push ourselves, given the will and desire to win. Every time I've come off the mat victorious, I've proven to myself and everyone who has seen it happen what I know to be true: anything is possible.

CHAPTER 12

Who I Am and What I Believe

'm grateful for the 15 minutes of fame I've received, but I'd be content in my life without it. I want to do my best to have a positive impact on people and I realize that media is necessary to do that. Coach Ramos was a very big believer that my story was worth telling to as many people as possible.

Like an army recruiter, Coach Ramos sent out many tapes of me wrestling before my senior season had started. He thought I deserved some type of recognition for the work I put in. I didn't necessarily think so, but he wanted to surprise me with a few things. He thought that I could be a role model to other kids and teach them the importance of staying positive with the belief that anything is possible. I hope I have had that effect. If nothing else, I try to live it.

As part of the exposure, HBO Real Pro Sports did a story which led to a host of media coverage and my becoming represented by the prestigious Washington Speakers Bureau. The Bureau markets me as a speaker to corporations, wellness conventions, and all types of schools.

Speaking to huge groups of people is one of the most amazing things I've ever felt. I get the same adrenaline rush as I do right before a wrestling match, and it's a great feeling to know that the people in the audience may take one or two things I said in the speech and apply it in their lives.

I was so nervous at my first couple of speeches, but that disappeared after I got to do much larger events like speaking to 15,000 kids, parents, and coaches at the AAU's Junior Olympics in Des Moines, Iowa.

Now I hope to continue speaking for the rest of my life to deliver the 'No Excuses' message to all types of people.

I've been asked why I wouldn't want to be a teacher, which is what most wrestling coaches choose to do for a living. But I feel that I have a responsibility to take every opportunity to have a positive impact on others through speaking and writing.

I was presented with an inspirational honor from the Sullivan AAU Committee in New York. It was here that I met aqua man, Olympian Michael Phelps. Even with six medals around his neck, you can't find a more humble guy than him. I was inspired by his work ethic as he was preparing for the 2004 Olympics. He agreed to come up to New York but said that he needed most of the day without distractions in the water to train. I felt bad for ever wanting to take a break myself.

Many newspapers, television shows, and magazines started paying attention to me; it was fun to hear the new questions that each reporter came up with, and meet new people in the process. Spike TV aired a documentary about my senior season and afterwards I got to visit the WWE when they came to Atlanta. I had the pleasure of meeting many of my childhood heroes, like Stone Cold Steve Austin, Shawn the Heartbreak Kid Michaels, Ric Flair, and Booker T. I even got to talk with Randy Orton about his old high school wrestling career.

In July I won the ESPY award for Best Athlete with a Disability. This was an award I had dreamt of winning since I was in junior high. It was unbelievable—and the best part was that I had the chance to represent an enormous community of disabled athletes across the country. There were a number of other spectacular people who deserved the award as much as I did, but I was honored to represent a community of fearless competitors.

I met the greatest athletes in the world in all sports. I felt like I was living a dream the entire time. But once again, it took an ESPY committee, event coordinator Jennifer Aielo, and over ten million online voters to make my dream a reality. So I want to thank all of you again who voted for me.

Luck continued to come my way as World Famous photographer, Bruce Weber, worked with me to do an article with Vanity Fair Magazine. After we had such a great shoot for the magazine, Bruce chose me as a model for an A & F Rising Star catalog.

It was so cool to get in front of the camera as a model. Bruce's crew made the process very enjoyable and the shoot was an awesome experience for me and my sister Amber who came with me as well. Bruce even chose to feature me in his book published with Nan Bush, All-American IV: Otherworldly, showcasing people who he believe have uniquely American characteristics.

A cover story appeared in USA Today in November of 2004. Marco della Cava wrote a terrific article after spending a lot of time with me and my family. He was there to watch my first wrestling match as a Georgia Bulldog. The response from readers was overwhelming. In fact, my website crashed!

Larry King read the article and invited me to do his show. I really couldn't imagine that this sort of thing would ever happen to me, and never thought I'd have the opportunity to experience that national stage.

On a more serious note, I received an email from one person who said they were literally preparing to commit suicide—but after seeing the Larry King show, they decided against taking their life. That was the single best reward I have ever received, and that kind of experience makes everything I do worth it.

While on the show, Larry discussed my driving situation. I had just received my driver's license a few months before, and he asked the television audience to help donate a vehicle that could be technically engineered for my personal use.

The problem was that I refused to drive a mini-van, not that I wasn't able to adapt to a specially-made vehicle. Mini-vans were the only vehicles my 250 pound electric wheelchair could fit in without being exposed to the elements outside.

My family and I already solved the actual driving issue by raising up the pedals with extensions so I could use my feet to drive. The steering wheel and controls remained the same as any other vehicle, but I pull the seat as close as I can to the wheel to have good control over it.

Driving was an issue I faced and had overcome, but I still didn't have a vehicle because I was reluctant to drive a mini-van. I assumed that I wouldn't have to drive a van if I held out long enough to find a way to adapt something better.

Not one, but many offers came my way for a vehicle. World renowned inventor and entrepreneur, Doc Watson of Heart International, a company that specializes in enabling people with disabilities, along with his son-in-law, Jimmy D. Dowsett II, agreed to custom make, and name a vehicle after me, the "KM Enabler." The vehicle looks more like a tank than a car!

In January 2005, Reader's Digest did a feature on me. They captured the true nature of my family and showed a picture of me wrestling my little sister Lindsay in the living room.

Good things continue to happen for me. I have been truly blessed. There's a little irony in my story because I had to believe in myself before everyone else could believe in me, but I never would have been able to have that personal faith if it wasn't for everyone helping me along the way.

I'm a competitor whose home is on the wrestling mat. I'd be as happy coaching wrestling as any other job in the world. Sometimes the media can portray people as weaker individuals who want to make people sympathetic towards them. The people I wrestle certainly aren't sympathetic. We share an unspoken connection on the mat which can't be described. We can feel each other's intensity.

I become a different person on the mat. I never would've gotten to be where I am today without a killer instinct. There's a switch that goes off in every true athlete's head when it's time to go. When I put on my singlet and strap my headgear, I adopt the animalistic attitude. My father taught me to be controlled, yet very aggressive. The controlled aggression doesn't relent until the match ends.

I feel more at home on the wrestling mat than anywhere else. I don't care what people say about me on the mat. The outcome is going to be the same anyway you cut it: I will do whatever needs to be done to win. I will win at any cost to my own or my opponent's body, because we both know before the match begins that wrestling isn't a meek sport.

Other wrestlers aren't discriminate in regards to lowering their efforts against me, because they know I'm coming after them the second the whistle blows. If anything, they'll try harder to stop from being beaten by a kid who rides a wheelchair.

Likewise, I don't differentiate between anyone I wrestle; on the mat I have to punish everyone. If I had to choose, I'd like to win by sleek style or finesse every bout, but the truth is at times I have to put my opposition in enough pain they want to pin themselves to end the match.

There are no special rules or courtesies I'm given over anyone else. I'm there to engage in combat and it's combat that drives me particularly hard. The blood in my veins isn't passive or submissive. My ancestors had the same appreciation for combat as I do.

My father's ancestors, the Keith Clan, came from the highlands in the castle Dunnottar. They were known for their warlike prowess and fought alongside William Wallace and Robert the Bruce for the independence of Scotland. My mother's ancestry is no different, with roots from the Cherokee Indians in Southeastern United States. They were no strangers to fighting for passion.

I love wrestling like nothing else I've experienced in my life. And, as a result I'm able to push myself harder as a wrestler than I can in any other aspect of my life.

It's not possible to be the very best at everything, and it's arrogant to even fathom it in anyone's life. But, we can focus on the one or two things that we love to do more than anything else. We can hone our skills in our particular area and dream about the sacrifice we're going to launch into and the challenges we'll face on the way.

My dad jokingly told me that he'd be disabled if he went up against Lebron James in a basketball game, because no one can expect to be the best at everything.

I've had a few people ask me why I pursue normalcy in my life, implying that I should accept the fact that I'm different from normal people.

Nature may have stripped me of my limbs but it only super sized my stubbornness. I hate to lose, but even more so, I detest giving in to the circumstances that are out of my control.

Why should I sit back and complain about life when I know I can get up off my butt and do the same things anyone else can do? I've chosen to live an active life because I want to experience everything life has to offer. Maybe it's because of the way I've been raised or because of the challenges I've already faced on a day-to-day basis, but I simply won't let any disability stand in my way.

I believe God only gives us challenges that He knows we are capable of handling. Whether we handle those challenges or not is up to us. We have the ability through free will and the capability to do anything if we allow ourselves to completely trust Him.

I model the way I compete after the very best. Randy Couture is one of the most dangerous fighters on the planet, but he's also one of the nicest guys I've ever met. He's a true Ultimate Fighting Championship warrior. Randy is methodical and doesn't stop. He drives his opponents from one end of the cage to the other, the same way I force my opposition off of the mat.

Randy was a world class wrestler who made the transition into the mixed martial arts scene. Since then, he's dominated in the UFC by using his 30-plus years of experience on the mat and he's shown how wrestling is as effective as any martial art.

Randy is 41 years old and competes against people who are barely over half his age. He overcomes the challenge of having an aged body with his relentless work ethic and his merciless attack. Outside of the cage he's a normal human being. He knows how to manipulate his intensity, but more importantly, he never takes the aggression beyond the competition—just the good qualities.

In the same way, I don't carry the over-aggressive traits of a wrestler's attitude with me off the mat. But the determination and concentration I've developed through the sport are two characteristics which have served me well in day-to-day life.

I accept the fact that I'll never be able to "Bend the ball like David Beckham," and I appreciate his incredible ability to do so, but I doubt he'll ever be able to hit a single leg takedown as quick as I can.

I've been blessed by certain things I can do very well and I thank God everyday for those blessings. I don't direct my concentration on the hundreds of wrestling moves I won't be able to execute in a match when I know that countless Olympians have been forged off of three or four moves which they perfect.

I find it important to laugh and that's how I get through the discouragements on a day-to-day basis. Pulling pranks are a great way to let other people around me know I'm comfortable with who I am.

In the summer after my freshman year in high school I went to a church retreat to the beach in Panama City, Florida with a few of my friends. We wanted to do something big in order to entertain us in between the camp's sessions, so we hatched a plan. One of my friends, a wrestling teammate, put on a poncho and a shark mask. Another friend of mine dressed up like a typical beach lifeguard. And we stopped by the dining hall to borrow a huge can of tomato purée.

Out on the beach, I swam out in the shallows and thrashed around with the "shark." The "lifeguard" did his best David Hasselhoff trot to the water. He pulled me out of the water and laid me on the sand while another friend came up and dumped the tomato purée on the ends of my arms and legs.

They started to yell out "Shark attack!" and drew the attention of everyone on the beach who came running up to see what had happened. I was lying in the sand and convulsing like a good stuntman. People were panic stricken around us, and my friends and I could barely contain our laughter—but we knew it was time to call the stunt off when one scared girl ran up the beach to call 911.

My attitude toward others is what allows me to sit back and not be focused in a negative way on my physical disability. I try to embrace people's curiosity instead of being enraged by it. There's nothing wrong with worrying about someone else. Sometimes it's hard for people to see past the disability and buy into my normalcy attitude.

I have a hard time convincing people that I am capable of more than it appears. My situation is unique in the sense that it is visually recognizable but not that much of a problem to live with at all.

I'm inspired by countless other individuals across the world who are amputees, one way or another, and continue about their lives in a totally normal way. My family and I have learned a great deal from such motivating people and we now provide confidence to other families by reassuring them that the future can be as bright as can be imagined.

I'm a normal guy off the mat and away from the weight room. I don't take on the same menacing grappler attitude except in competition. Even my grades in school tell the tale. I finished high school with a 3.7 GPA, but I'm sure it could've easily been a 4.0, had I invested more time and effort. Instead, I chose to focus on other things I feel are important too.

Don't forget, I have the same emotions as anyone else. I know how it feels to be shattered at times. I've questioned God and why He made me the way I am. I've learned certain things won't be understood until later on in life, whereas others aren't ever meant to be comprehended. We just need to accept God and His plans for our lives.

I have the same types of troubles in my life as other people do. I have more issues with relationships and women than anything else. I date about as much as anyone else my age, but I'm always hoping to find the perfect girl for me to spend the rest of my life with.

I'm a hopeless romantic. I end up feeling like I could fall in love with anyone at anytime. I treat the women I'm with as best as I know how, but the real issue is finding someone who truly looks at me without any disability.

It's difficult to carry on a romance and appear like any normal couple when you have an obvious physical difference. And it's not just difficult for me or the girl I'm dating to feel normal, but for everyone surrounding us as well.

Someday soon I'll have a wife and children of my own. I know genetics have nothing to do with my situation, but I can't say I wouldn't fear any type of adversity in my child's life. My parents were barely older than I am now at the time I was born, yet they managed to see the light in my life before anyone else.

Not knowing won't keep me from having that family of my own. I hope my children never face a life with the same type of adversity that I've experienced, but I have no doubt that such experiences will help anyone grow. I've never allowed my disability to stand in front of me and what I ultimately want.

LIVING WITH NO EXCUSES

During the summer before my senior year in high school, my best friend Joey Leonardo, his girlfriend and the girl I was interested in at the time all took a trip to visit our favorite amusement park, Six Flags Over Georgia.

We started the trip off by picking up 4 season pass coupons at the grocery store and made the hour and a half drive to the park. We stood in the lines, got our picture taken for our season passes and we were chatting about all of the rides we planned to go to see.

When we walked into the park we headed towards the closest rollercoaster, the Georgia Scorcher, which happened to be a ride you need to stand upright for. We talked to one of the park's managers at the ride and he was totally cool with letting me on.

I told him that I'd been to the park several times before and hadn't had a problem dealing with anything. He even said he was going to radio everyone around the park to let them know I was on the way and they shouldn't worry about me.

We rode the standup rollercoaster and had a blast. We were talking about how much fun the last ride was up until we arrived at the next one. We stood in line and watched everybody walk away with smiles on their faces. I've always loved roller coasters because of the rush I get from riding them.

There was a bit of a problem once we finally got to the front of the line and were ready to get on the ride.

I was ready to jump out of my wheelchair and head up to the ride until a lady started to approach us. She was curious if I had verified with anyone else about riding the rides and I told her the truth, which was that we discussed it with the manager at the other roller coaster.

This next ride was even safer for me, or anyone else for that matter, to ride in the first place. It was a seat with a shoulder-harness and a lap bar on top of that. I could sit down in the seat and I'd have to be studying under Houdini to get out of the thing.

The lady wasn't convinced that I'd be safe, so she called a supervisor up to assess the situation. I was fine with that, as I figured we'd gotten away too easily after the first ride and I wanted to resolve the issue that I'd be safe on the shoulder-harness rides. That way we wouldn't be forced to go through the same hassle every time we went to a new ride.

We waited for quite a while as the supervisor walked from one end of the park in his office to the other side where we were. I told my friends they could go ahead and get on the ride but they decided not to. We stayed optimistic and joked around with each other while the supervisor came up.

He wasn't able to come to a conclusive decision when he finally arrived thirty minutes after we did, so we waited close to an additional hour after that. My friends were still optimistic with me, but I was frustrated by the fact that they refused to go on the ride without me. I would've been alright waiting there as long as they were having a good time, but I felt bad holding everyone up.

When the supervisor's supervisor showed up, he was noticeably exhausted. I could tell he was very overweight and I thought we could connect on that level. I feel as though weight is an overlooked challenge which people have to overcome, just like my own circumstances. I was sure he'd come across some type of dilemma where someone misjudged his ability as a consequence of his weight issue.

If that was the case, then I assumed he'd be sympathetic towards my situation and let us go on the rides as I had before.

As he got closer I noticed it was the same person who had cleared me to do all of the rides at the park (except one ride without the shoulder-harness) six months prior. Now I was completely sure we'd get everything squared away and could pickup our day where we left off.

Instead, he was reluctant to allow me onto the ride because I didn't meet the criteria of a capable person. He explained I needed three limbs with joints before I could ride.

I told him I have four limbs with joints: my two shoulders and hips. But, he wouldn't accept that and ended up changing the criteria to three limbs with an additional joint, such as an elbow or knee. He suggested I come back and wear my prosthetics next time.

I told him I wasn't able to move at all if I was wearing prosthetics. The prosthetics completely disabled me.

I pleaded my case with the man. I told him I'd have a 350 pound death grip on the shoulder-harness, on top of the fact that the force pushing me into the seat would make it nearly impossible to escape anyway.

Ironically, right as he started to suggest to me that I should be wearing prosthetics, I noticed a delay in the ride's movement. There was an adult man on the same ride who was being helped off by his sons.

I saw two of the boys lift and carry the man from the seat on the rollercoaster to his wheelchair waiting on the side of the ride. At first glance I was excited to see someone else in a wheelchair outside and enjoying life. Everyone they were with was smiling and talking about how cool the ride was.

This man was just as big of a risk on that ride as I was, if not more. I commented to the supervisors there to watch how the man had no mobility at all in his limbs, yet he was allowed to ride by the regulations and I was not.

I didn't even want to have to make the comparison between the paralyzed man and myself but I reluctantly inquired as to what would happen if the ride was stuck and everyone had to walk off. They answered by saying they'd try to get the man assistance.

I told them I'd been wrestling for up to 6 years at that point and had no problems with mobility whatsoever and again tried to reassure them there was no way I was falling out of this completely safe ride.

I understood their reasoning, whether or not I agreed with it, which was if I happened to slip out of the ride they'd be accountable. I tried to work around that by asking to sign some type of document, but even then they were unwilling to compromise.

Now my friends started to step into the fray by getting upset at the park's management and began asking why the place's policies had changed all of the sudden. The kids I was with saw me as I see myself; without any difference at all.

The park said the policy hadn't changed and the only reason I was allowed to ride so many times before was due to communication errors.

I finally snapped—I was at the end of my rope and felt I had been too patient with the supervisors. I answered all of their questions and provided them with a plethora of reasons to let me on the thing. It began as a pointless argument, but now it was a matter of pride.

I was absolutely embarrassed and was bursting with emotion on the inside. I couldn't stand what was going on here because after hearing firsthand their practiced speeches I had a feeling they must pull this argument against a lot of other physically challenged people. I felt powerless to change what they were doing to us and I knew what was going to happen. They wouldn't let me ride and we'd have to spend the afternoon arguing to no end without a resolution.

I was most embarrassed by the fact that I was with a beautiful girl, Alexandria, and two of my other closest friends in the world and here the supervisors were singling me out. For one of the first times in my life I truly felt what it was like to be discriminated against because of something I couldn't control.

The park supervisors were wrong, in my opinion, but we all know why they behaved the way they did. It's because the law makes cowards of mid-level bureaucrats by holding the threat of lawsuits over their heads.

Many of us, in our daily lives, have various annoying bureaucrats we have to deal with, who tend to work in jobs for the government or insurance companies or other similar areas. Even at my young age I've noticed that this trend is spreading rapidly. In fact, I'd say that today, the increasing legal foolishness and bureaucratization of American life is one of the chief factors undercutting the "No Excuses" worldview that I preach and live.

To live with "No Excuses" means to take a robust, rugged individualistic attitude toward life's problems; it's about freedom and responsibility; it's about hard work and hard choices; it's about self-reliance that is joined naturally with family, friends, community and faith. No excuses is about America as it used to be and should always be.

That's part of what I stand for. And it added to my frustration with the park supervisors on that day in Georgia. Of course, it was also a deeply personal embarrassment for me because I was with a girl I really liked, and I felt like I was being humiliated by someone who didn't look at me as a fully capable human being, but as something less. When they were confronted on it, they hid sniveling behind their bureaucratic rulebooks.

I wanted the supervisors to apologize and be more understanding. If we could come to an agreement, I was confident they'd let me on. If they still wouldn't let me on, then I could have a better chance convincing my friends to go on without me.

I finally got to the point where I didn't care if I was on the ride or not—all I wanted was closure. The managers continued to be rude and I became very frustrated.

I drew the attention of almost 200 people standing in line for the rollercoaster by leaping out of my wheelchair and shadow wrestling for a second before I threw my body up in the air to do a walking handstand.

It was a physical display of my capability to back up everything I was claiming in case they were sleeping through my side of the story. I started yelling out and questioning if a kid who didn't meet their requirements could do the handstand push-ups like I was doing.

The supervisors noticed how people were rallying to my cause and yelling to let me on the ride. Everyone was in support of letting me on the ride and I felt rebellious enough to offer a challenge.

Where most people would've walked away or considered legal action for the emotional duress suffered from the whole encounter, I chose differently.

I called them out by audibly asking if any of them would like to try and stop me from getting on the ride. If they could physically keep me off of the ride after a struggle, then I'd be all right with walking away. But, if I was able to show dominance by running through their biggest supervisor, then I figured it'd be appropriate to let me on the ride.

Other men around me voiced their support, but I felt as if I'd made a mistake. I should've been a bigger person and not tested their patience.

On the other hand, if you've read anything up to this point, then I'm guessing you understand I'm not the guy who usually backs away. I was hoping one of the park's supervisors would brave up to the challenge, but it was an exercise in futility.

I was still disappointed when my friends declined to stay at the park and have fun after I pleaded with them to do so. I would've felt better if they had a good time, and it would've lessened the blow to my confidence if the situation was forgotten.

But they embodied everything I could ever ask for out of a friendship, as they decided to stick with me and oppose going on the rides if I couldn't.

I have always felt a strong kinship to anyone who stands up to any type of noticeable adversity. I'd be willing to try and help someone who needs a break over someone who doesn't based upon on the experiences I've had throughout my life.

I wanted to stand up right then and there to come to blows for every indecent thing that's ever been done to another human being. I wanted to be an activist for every voice which needed help yelling. I wanted to be the sword that tore through the disgraces of prejudiced behavior in our society.

I learned that day about the true incapability of specific people who can't get past differences in every human being. There was no reason, other than policy, which kept me from getting on the rollercoaster. Misunderstood policy that was a product of miscommunication since I'd already slipped through their cracks two times before within the last year.

I felt the injustice leaking out of this policy but I wasn't going to let it stop me. We filed our formal customer complaint, got our money back for the season tickets, and drove home. I didn't let the trip stop me in trying to pursue a relationship with Alex or stop Joey and Krissi from believing in me.

My parents were infuriated by what transpired and we considered legal action against the park, but decided against it. I'd gotten my point across and I had nothing else to say. I let the bad blood simmer down and rinse away. I told myself that someday I'd show up with a couple of powerful enough societal leaders to waltz by the supervisors and get back on those rides.

In retrospect, I know that I was too aggressive that day at the park. But it's in my nature to sometimes not know when I need to stop. I want to keep fighting, but oftentimes that's not the best way to learn and grow as a person. Everyone goes beyond the limits once in a while, and we reach a point where things become personally destructive.

That's a balance we all have to learn. Yet at the same time, we should never shy away from the challenges that face us out of fear of failure or an unwillingness to battle the odds. We should confront our problems head on, and make no excuses.

That's one of the reasons I wear a tiger tattoo on my shoulder. You can see it on the front of this book. It serves as a reminder to have a tiger's heart, to never quit, to never back down to anyone or anything, to fear no challenge. A tiger's heart is sometimes savage and aggressive, but it is also noble and brave—and in the end, no matter what happens in the outside world, it is victorious. I wear this tattoo to remind me to fight every battle to the end—that's the essence of who I am and what I believe.

"We make our own luck. We decide our own fate."

- Dan Gable

No Excuses.

My high school wrestling career climaxed in the Georgia state wrestling tournament. I had the opportunity to wrestle in my weight class as one of the toughest thirty-two wrestlers in the state. I had a record of 35 wins and 16 losses my senior year—the same number of wins as the number of losses that started my wrestling career.

My first round opponent was a wrestler I had beaten once and lost to once. In the pre-tournament predictions, the prognosticators said that I'd lose in the first round.

I focused on this contest the entire week leading up to the match, running it through my head as I sat in class and in the darkness before I fell asleep at night. I watched the tape where I had lost before with Coach Ramos, I worked on my conditioning, and I knew what I had to do.

My family and I drove through the calm Georgia night to get ready before the tournament began. While we drove, I thought about my conversation with Dan Gable only a week earlier. I told him that I would need a lot of luck to pull out a win at the state championship. Coach Gable said: "We make our own luck. We decide our own fate." And I knew it was up to me whether I'd come out on top.

My teammates and I checked out the Macon Centreplex together to get used to the site of our coming bouts. The place was empty except for a few wrestlers rolling on the mats and a few tournament workers who were washing the place down with mat cleanser. The distinct antiseptic smell wafted through the air. The arena seemed vast; the floor contained a full twelve mats, where most High School competitions only hold three, and there were stadium seats for thousands of spectators.

My teammates and I spent the night taking turns running on the hotel's lone treadmill. I wasn't nervous about the matches the next day, but I felt my anxiety growing. I wanted to start the match already—I wanted to face the challenge and win.

The next day was a blur of preparation as I got ready for the first round match. My opponent was cutting weight in order to stay in this class, and I knew he didn't have the discipline to do it efficiently without losing strength. But after the whistle blew, he scored the first points of the match, a second period reversal that broke the 0-0 deadlock. He went up on me 2-0. But after I scored an escape, I could tell that he was weakening and dehydrated. It wasn't long before I scored a takedown to take the lead in the match with a 3-2 score.

My third period escape sealed the match for good. It was a sweet 4-2 victory.

I was on an emotional high after winning the match, and I had a forty-five minute break before I faced my next opponent. Deep down, I didn't even know if I would make it past that first match—others certainly hadn't thought I could—so in those moments of calm, I started to lose my focus.

My next match pitted me against someone I had previously dominated by a large margin. It appeared as though I was in complete control in the third period with thirty seconds left to go. I had scored three takedowns from single legs and he scored three escapes from the bottom. I was ahead by a score of 6-3, and I had the upper hand.

The match should have been all but over, but I became anxious as he went wild to score a takedown. His motions were frantic, and I was nervous—the kid wasn't a great wrestler, but he was absolutely intense. I wanted to ride it out, weathering the storm for thirty seconds more.

In retrospect, the smart tactic would've been to let my opponent get a takedown. That way he would only get 2 points, and I would've only had to stay in position for fifteen seconds until the match was over. But as always, I was stubborn, and I refused to let him get a takedown.

Instead I tried a peek-out—one of my best moves, that had worked hundreds of times before,—and won me match after match during the year—but my opponent guessed it was coming, and counter-attacked. He whipped me to my back to score a takedown and three near-fall points.

Thanks to that one mistake, I had lost the lead, and now I knew I couldn't get it back. After I scored an escape to make it 8-7, he just backed away and won the match.

I had never felt so horrible from a loss in all the years I'd wrestled. My opponent went on to win his quarter-finals match by a technical fall, which is the fifteen point mercy rule, and he wrestled in the semi-finals the following morning.

I knew that my team needed me to make a comeback and perform well in the wrestle-backs, even though my dreams of becoming a state champion were gone. A wrestle-back bracket is effectively the loser's bracket, as most wrestling tournaments are double elimination. I was frustrated, but I couldn't allow my emotions to overwhelm me. I couldn't let my team down.

My opposition in the first round of wrestle-backs paired me with a regional competitor who was tall, lanky, and had a serious rivalry with me. I had wrestled him repeatedly since ninth grade, and I had never lost to him, but this match was close throughout.

He clearly had a game plan going in, and scored the first takedown on me to lead 2-1 in the second period. We both scored escapes—but in the third period he was called for stalling twice, and it sent the match into overtime with a 3-3 teeth-gnashing gridlock between two seniors who didn't want to end their seasons early.

He was a lot longer than most opponents I wrestled, and it was tough to get leverage when he was holding my head down. But he was mentally fatigued after the early match, and he began to be overaggressive as we started the sudden death overtime.

I saw the window of opportunity I needed. I continued to pressure him, and when he couldn't back up any longer, he had to press into me. I used his momentum, leveraged my body against his, and used the peek-out move. His body flipped, and I scored a takedown. The victory was mine by a score of 5-3.

I stepped off the mat and got some fluids. I went and weighed myself, knowing that I had to make weight that night—but I found that I was nine pounds overweight. I hoped that wouldn't be a problem, and that I'd cut most of the weight during my next match.

My last match of the night paired me with a younger opponent who was strong and fast. I knew I had to use my patience and experience to edge him.

This opponent was a lot to handle. With a flurry of scoring in the second and third periods, he led 6-4 with less than a minute to go.

He was exhausted towards the end of the third period, off balance and tentative in his movements, and my intense conditioning allowed me to think clearly. So I shot in deep on a single leg, trying to score a takedown.

Instead, he crushed my broken nose with a gruesome crossface, slamming his arm against me, sending blood pouring down the back of my throat.

I started to fade out but tried to grip the leg as hard as I possibly could. I eventually got hold of his opposite ankle to score the two points for a takedown, tying the match at 6-6 and sending my second consecutive match into overtime.

I knew before my opponent came to the center circle that he had pushed himself as hard as he was going to in the third period. He was dog-tired when the overtime started, and I was weakened too.

I worked in on a low single-leg shot near his ankle. He collapsed his weight on top of me in a last ditch effort to keep me from scoring.

The crowd of family and friends from my high school started chanting my name, and I felt a burst of adrenaline. I knew that finishing that takedown was all that kept me from a rematch with the kid who had beaten me in the regional tournament finals. I felt my heart race as I circled around his side, holding on for dear life, and eventually he lost his balance. I had the two point score and an 8-6 overtime conquest.

After the match, I weighed myself again. I had dropped four pounds just thanks to the exertion and sweat—but I was still five pounds over with little more than thirty minutes to weigh in. I had to cut that weight, and fast. So I put on as many heavy clothes and sweats as I could, and went out to a friend's SUV in the parking lot which had heated seats. I blasted the hot air and turned the seats full on as I did jumping jacks and ran around, sweating profusely. With just minutes to spare, I made the weight.

That night, I got a call from my wrestling hero, Cael Sanderson. He congratulated me on winning three matches in my first day at the state tournament. He knew I had a tough match in the morning, but told me not to let the pressure of winning get to me. I took his words to heart as I prepared for the next day's showdown.

My last match as a Collins Hill Eagle appropriately put me against a wrestler from our toughest regional rival, the Parkview Panthers. I had faced Parkview's 103 pounder three times and only had one victory to show for it.

I knew that he'd beaten me before, and that if he beat me again, I'd be out of the tournament, and my High School career would be over. Coach Ramos and I had prepared for this possibility—we'd watched film on this opponent, even though I didn't know if I'd wrestle him at all.

Our strategy was simple but challenging. Coach Ramos told me to use the boundary and my position on the mat to my advantage. I knew this opponent would be attacking my face, and that if I used the boundary well, I could frustrate him and cause him to make mistakes.

This wrestler had developed a strategy to beat me. His teammates had practiced with him before the match, staying on their knees so he could practice wrestling someone of my stature.

As the match began, I felt his strategy, and it was effective. He used his jagged forearm to hook my broken nose. That helped him gain control of my head. He threw his weight against me and tried to score a takedown. I could choose to fight back, risk getting pinned, or let him score the 2 points—which I did.

I now knew his strategy, but that didn't help the throbbing pain of my smashed nose.

He scored two takedowns in the first period. I escaped both times by getting control of his arms and clearing them away from my body, freeing my hips from under him. The score was 4-2.

He chose the bottom position in the second period, and got an escape halfway through to make the score 5-2. He continued to go to work on my face, and we scrambled out of bounds repeatedly without either of us getting control.

I knew I was behind, and I was desperate to score a takedown. I tried to reach his legs, but I couldn't take much more punishment to the front of my face. As I suffered yet another shot to my face, I dropped my head to fend off the blow.

I'd made an error, and my opponent capitalized on it. He twisted around behind me, keeping my head stuffed to the ground. I could feel his legs brush by the ends of my arms, and for a moment, I just wished I had an extra inch of arm to grip onto him.

It was 7-2 at the end of the second period. My head had made contact with his, and opened up his eyebrow, so we both tried to clean our faces of blood.

In the third, we were totally fatigued and drenched in sweat, and our reaction times were slower. I initially chose the bottom, and quickly escaped to make the score 7-3. But then as I drove him toward the boundary, he slammed his forearm on my nose again, cranking my neck and getting close enough to score a takedown. It was 9-3.

I kept telling myself that I had to score, no matter the pain, that otherwise this was the end. I saw an opening when my opponent put too much body weight on one foot. I dove for his ankle and locked it between my chin and shoulder, using his knee as a fulcrum.

I scored the reversal to make it 9-5. I could feel it—I was coming back.

Then, as I was gripped on behind him, and he was on all fours, he started kicking my face. He pounded on my exposed nose with his wrestling shoe, causing the most excruciating pain I've felt in my life. The ref couldn't see what was happening from his vantage point, so he didn't stop it. Blood ran down my throat as I held on like a vice, trying to bring him down.

Somehow, even in the mist of blood and pain, I got control of his other leg and brought his hips down to the mat enough so that I could snake up his body. With his hips flat, he posted his right arm up, trying to do a pushup to lift his stomach off the ground.

That was all I needed. I ripped at his elbow, trying to pull his arm behind his back like a chicken wing. I took my left arm and dug it into his back, and I could feel him wince in pain.

Less than fifteen seconds were left. I was down by four points. My only chance was to get the pin.

I tried to use my right arm to bend his back arm around, and raked my left arm into his chin, trying to pull him onto his back. I almost had him.

But then his arm slipped away from me, and he escaped. He ran away from me around the edge of the mat. I couldn't get close enough to him to pin.

The final seconds drained off the clock. The referee blew his whistle. The final score was 10-5.

My season and my high school career were over.

We came back to the center of the mat and shook hands. My opponent dropped down to his knees to embrace me. He told me that we'd had one of the best battles he'd ever experienced, and I agreed. The next year, he went undefeated.

He walked off the mat, and I sat there, still quietly stunned. It seemed like an eternity, alone at the center circle.

I saw Coach Ramos coming toward me, the one person who'd had the biggest impact in bringing me to this point. The man who taught me to never accept failure picked me up off the ground, lifted me in his arms, and carried me off the mat.

As Coach Ramos carried me, I saw so many of the people who had been heroes to me: my parents, family, grandparents and friends. I could see the sorrow and the tears—but also the smiles as they stood up and clapped. I saw the pride in my father's face for getting this far and giving my all.

And then I heard the applause—not just from my school, but from the Panthers as well, from hundreds of people who'd seen me wrestle over so many years, who'd seen me struggle and win. They stood and cheered. It was deafening.

In that moment, I understood I'd had a deeper impact than I ever could've imagined. I'd accomplished my goal. I knew in my heart that all the training, all the hard work, all the passion hadn't been in vain.

Even in defeat, I knew I had won.

Acknowledgements

This book is a tribute to the people I love, their indomitable character, and fearless attitudes which have affected my life in extraor-
dinary ways. My life to date and in the future are forever entwined
with their love and support.

Foremost, I thank my parents for plenty of tough love blended
with compassion when I needed it most. My parents, Scott and Anita,
have shaped the perfect example of the home every kid should grow
up in.

My sisters, Amber, Lindsay, and MacKenzie, have the sweetest
hearts of anyone I've ever known. We're always there to support one
another, and I will forever cherish my special relationships with each
one of them.

Thanks to my grandparents, aunts, uncles, and cousins for their love, humor, and strength. I am blessed to be around so many wonderful people who love God as much as I do.

Thanks to my closest friends, who are always beside me and supportive of everything I fight for. They are exceptional friends who have been a part of molding who I have become. I thank them all for being themselves and allowing me to do the same.

I thank my close friend and manager, Tony Marinozzi, for having the type of relentless grit and work ethic that I greatly respect. Without Tony, I would've never been given the opportunity to reach so many people through the opportunities I've been given, which is exactly why God has put him in my life. "Commit to the Lord whatever you do, and your plans will succeed. (Proverbs 16:3)"

Thanks to the first-rate people working at Regnery. I didn't know what I was getting myself into when they first approached me about the book, but since then, I've made some very special friends. I especially thank Jeff Carneal, who has been a friend who has taught me a lot and one I won't ever forget. This book wouldn't have been possible without the faith Marji Ross and Harry Crocker have in me. I particularly want to thank my editor, Ben Domenech, and the rest of the Regnery team who worked on this book—Kristen Schremp, Christine Klima, and Angela Phelps. Regnery is full of special people, and I've come to consider many of them to be close friends.

I give special thanks to the wrestling community of competitors, coaches, and parents for continuing to have an impact on so many lives. I have no idea where my life would be without the sport and the lessons I've learned through it.

Finally, a very special thank you to one of my closest friends and mentor, Coach Cliff Ramos. Without his guidance and knowledge, I would've been lost. It's hard to express the extent of my gratitude to one of the most influential people I've ever known.

Every day, I thank Jesus Christ for the blessings He has given me now and for the eternal life we all can live in Heaven for believing in Christ. I truly believe that "I can do all things through Him who strengthens me. (Philippians 4:13)"

APPENDIX I Diet & Exercise Regimen

DIET PLAN

The general diet I follow during the off-season differs from the diet I keep to during the wrestling season. Even though I still compete and practice a good bit during the summer's off-season, I try to maximize my ability to gain mass.

The meals I choose to eat fluctuate from day-to-day, but the pattern remains the same. My diet is higher in carbohydrates and calories during the off-season to keep my weight at or under 120 lbs. Most diets recommend eating more than three meals a day, but that makes it hard to keep up with a busy schedule. I choose to eat 3 meals a day with a snack between lunch and dinner.

I always stick exactly with the diet I follow during the wrestling season, so I leave a little room for slip-ups with the off-season diet.

OFF-SEASON DIET – MUSCLE BULKING PHASE

- **BREAKFAST:** 3 scrambled egg whites, 2 sausage or bacon strips, 1 banana, 1 yogurt, 16 oz. glass of orange juice, multi-vitamin
- **LUNCH:** 1 ham or turkey sandwich with wheat bread, high protein energy bar (low in sugar), garden salad with romaine lettuce and olive oil dressing, 1 apple or orange, 12 oz. can of diet lemonade
- **SNACK:** high protein and carbohydrate shake mixed in 16 oz. glass of water, pretzels
- **DINNER:** 1 serving of brown rice or sweet potato without condiments, grilled chicken or fish, green vegetable or corn, dessert in moderation, 16 oz. glass of water

My mid-season diet makes a large reduction in my general consumption. During my senior season, I needed to weigh-in at 103 lbs. I devote a lot more time to my cardiovascular endurance during this time of year, which allows me to eat as much as I do. I choose to eat and exercise the extra calories away, while other wrestlers choose a less healthy approach and want to skip out on the exercise by not eating much at all. I make an extra effort to stay away from carbonated drinks during the season.

MID-SEASON DIET – BODY LEANING PHASE

▸ **BREAKFAST:** 1 serving of oatmeal prepared with skim milk and topped with 2 tbsp. of apple sauce for flavor, 16 oz. glass of water, multi-vitamin

▸ **LUNCH:** high protein energy bar low in sugar, 12 oz. can of diet lemonade

▸ **SNACK:** 3 separate pieces of lunch meat rolled up with low fat cheese

▸ **DINNER:** garden salad with romaine lettuce and low fat ranch or Italian dressing, small amount of grilled chicken or fish, 16 oz. glass of water

WORKOUT REGIMEN

Since the 6th grade, I've developed a series of movements using chains to attach free-weights to my arms. My workouts consist of varying levels of intensity and they cover every part of my body. I lift with a partner who helps me load the weights on the chains and slide them onto my arms. Consequently, I don't want to hassle my partner with changing the weight multiple times in one workout. At the beginning of every workout, I choose to do either heavier weight with lower reps or a higher rep workout with lower weight.

Once again, my workouts are affected by my wrestling schedule. My workout regimen follows the same pattern as my diet, with the same bulking and leaning phases. Off-season workouts devote more time in the gym towards strength and mass development by combining heavier weights with lower reps. I focus on having larger rest intervals, generally one week, after working a muscle group hard during the off-season.

During the middle of the wrestling season, I can't afford any increases in my mass if I hope to make weight, so I choose to concentrate on lower weights with higher repetitions. I rest my individual muscle groups about 2–3 days during the mid-season after a tough workout. This way I can enhance my muscular endurance.

I find it very important to stretch well before I pick up a weight. I've never had a super-serious injury in the weight room, and I attribute that to having a good warm-up routine. Stretching is a matter of preference, but it's imperative to stretch the body parts you are going to be using to lift. I spend 5–7 minutes stretching, followed by 3–5 minutes of push-ups, unweighted squats, or neck bridging.

My workouts only last 60–75 minutes at the most. I know what I need to do before I step inside the weight room, and I can socialize after the workout is finished.

I'll make a list of exercises I use every week and the ways I perform them in order to avoid confusion. I've modeled my movements after normal motions. I have put multiple teammates through my workouts, and they find them to be very effective, depending on the intensity and effort put into each movement.

Throughout the past eight years I've trained hard with weights, I have won multiple powerlifting competitions. In 2004 at GNC's Show of Strength in Atlanta, Georgia, I set the Unofficial World's Strongest Teen Title by lifting 240 lbs. for 23 repetitions in the Butterfly (modified bench press) at the 103 lbs. weight class. In March of 2005 at the Arnold Classic Fitness Expo in Columbus, Ohio, I broke the World Record for the Modified Bench Press by butterflying 360 lbs. as a maximum in the 125 lbs. weight class. At the same competition, I performed my personal best for repetitions by lifting 210 lbs. for 35 reps twice in an hour.

EXERCISE EXPLANATIONS

- **BENT-OVER ROWS:** I lie on top of a bench, flat on my stomach, resting my arms, weighted by the chains, straight down to the floor. I pull the weighted chains attached to my arms to a parallel position with the floor for one repetition.

    MAX: 160 lbs. (80 lbs. per arm) for 5 reps.

- **BUTTERFLY (MODIFIED BENCH PRESS):** I lie on top of a bench, flat on my back, extending my arms straight out and away from my sides. My arms are attached to weighed down chains on each side and begin the motion at 0 degrees/parallel to the floor. I lift both arms up until they pass 90 degrees/perpendicular to the floor—straight up towards the ceiling.

MAX: 360 lbs. (180 lbs. per arm) competition best, 410 lbs. personal best

▶   CHAIR DIPS: I place two chairs near me, with one on either side. I use my chest and shoulders to pull my body into the air, with only the ends of my arms touching the chairs in a dip motion. The full extension of my arms and back down counts for one repetition.

▶   CRUCIFIX (SIDE RAISES): I sit flat on the floor with my back straight and arms extended to my sides as far as I can. My arms are attached to the weighted chains, and I lift from 0 degrees to 90 degrees pointing at the ceiling.

MAX: 180 lbs. (90 lbs. per arm) for 3 reps

▶   CRUNCHES: Normal crunch motion to strengthen my abs. I do not extend all the way to be considered a full sit-up.

MAX: 76 reps in 60 seconds

▶   DELTOID SHRUGS: I sit flat on a bench towards the 45 lbs. straight bar. I rest the straight bar across my deltoids (shoulders) and lift in an arc motion. I drive the weights up with my deltoids and trapezius.

MAX: 315 lbs. for 8 reps

▶ **DRILLING WRESTLING MOVES:** Great cardiovascular improvements can come from drilling wrestling moves with a partner for speed and technique.

▶ **FLUTTER KICKS:** I lie flat on my back and keep my legs 6-10 inches off the ground. I kick my legs one at a time at increasing speeds for abdominal work.

▶ **FRONT DUMBBELL PRESS:** I sit flat on the floor and hold one end of a dumbbell between my two arms. I lift the dumbbell from my waist to my head.
   MAX: 120 lbs. for 15 reps

▶ **FRONT PLATE RAISES:** Similar to Front Dumbbell Press, but a 45 lbs. plate is laid flat across the ends of my arms and the plate is used instead of a dumbbell to change the shape of the object in motion.
   Max: 45 lbs. for 72 reps

▶ **GOOD MORNINGS:** I hang off the end of a bench press with a partner holding my legs down. I begin with the exercise with my forehead on the ground and finish when I extend my back and head as far as I can upwards. The reverse motion of bending over an object.
   MAX: 31 reps

▶ **JUMPING JACKS:** Normal jumping jacks to improve cardiovascular condition.

▶ **LEG LIFTS:** I lie flat on my back and raise my lower body off the floor to strengthen my abdominals.

▶ **LUNGES:** I stand up and extend one leg forward as I squat down. I return to a normal standing position and resume with the opposite leg. It's difficult cardiovascular work even to stand in a normal posture, since I usually walk on all fours or sit.
   MAX: 21 reps in 60 seconds

▶ **MEDICINE BALL SQUATS AND TOSSES:** Begins in the standing posture and drops down to a squat and back up while holding onto a 15 lbs. medicine ball. Then the ball is thrown in the air as high as I can toss it and caught before another squat rep.

▶ **PULL-UPS:** I attach my arm chains to the top bar in a squat rack and hang like a gymnast with the rings.

▶ **PUSH-UPS:** I begin by planting both arms and feet down with my head parallel to the floor. I lift with my shoulders and raise my entire body off the ground; only the ends of my arms remain in contact with the floor.
   MAX: 323 reps without breaking

▸ **SHADOW WRESTLING:** Constant motion in wrestling stance for cardiovascular work.

▸ **SPRINTS (BEARCRAWLS):** Sprinting on all fours, similar to the way a bear runs.

▸ **SQUATS:** I sit under a straight bar and rest it across my shoulders, holding it in place with my neck. I lift my body from a seated position to a normal standing posture and slowly back down for a single repetition.

   MAX: 155 lbs. for 5 reps

EXERCISE SCHEDULE

MUSCLE BULKING PHASE—WRESTLING OFF-SEASON: HIGHER WEIGHT AND LOWER REPS

Day of the Week—Body Part Worked	Exercise Sets Reps Weights				
Monday's Chest Workout	Butterfly 4 Sets 6 Reps 290 lbs	Chair Dips 3 Sets 12 Reps	Ball Tosses 5 min	Sprints 25 min	Crunches 250 Reps
Tuesday's Legs Workout	Squats 4 Sets 4 Reps 130 lbs	Ball Squats 3 Sets 20 Reps	Lunges 2 Sets 15 Reps	Swimming 35 min	
Wednesday's Back Workout	Bent-Over Rows 4 Sets 4 Reps 135 lbs	Pull-Ups 10 min	Good Mornings 3 Sets 15 Reps	Shadow Wrestling 20 min	
Thursday's Abdominal Workout	Leg Lifts 5 Sets 20 Reps	Flutter Kicks 5 Sets 2 min Each 30 Sec Rests	Crunches 250 Reps	Sprints 30 min	
Friday's Shoulder Workout	Front Plate Raises 4 Sets 25 Reps 45 lbs	Front Dumbbell Raises 2 Sets 8 Reps 130 lbs	Crucifix 4 Sets 6 Reps 130 lbs	Deltoid Shrugs 3 Sets 8 Reps 250 lbs	
Saturday's Cardiovascular Workout	Jumping Jacks 8 min	Shadow Wrestling 12 min	Sprints 20 min	Drilling Moves 30 min	
Sunday's Day of Rest and Relaxation					

EXERCISE SCHEDULE
BODY LEANING PHASE—WRESTLING SEASON: HIGHER REPS AND LOWER WEIGHT

Day of the Week—Body Part Worked	Exercise Sets Reps Weights				
Monday's Chest Workout	Butterfly 12 Sets 15 Reps 210 lbs	Chair Dips 5 Sets 8 Reps	Ball Tosses 5 min	Sprints 25 min	Crunches 250 Reps
Tuesday's Legs Workout	Squats 8 Sets 12 Reps 100 lbs	Ball Squats 3 Sets 20 Reps	Lunges 3 Sets 15 Reps	Swimming 35 min	
Wednesday's Back Workout	Bent-Over Rows 10 Sets 12 Reps 90 lbs	Pull-Ups 10 min	Good Mornings 4 Sets 12 Reps	Shadow Wrestling 20 min	
Thursday's Abdominal Workout	Leg Lifts 8 Sets 10 Reps	Flutter Kicks 8 Sets 1 min Each 30 Sec Rests	Crunches 250 Reps	Sprints 30 min	
Friday's Shoulder Workout	Front Plate Raises 10 Sets 12 Reps 45 lbs	Front Dumbbell Raises 5 Sets 5 Reps 80 lbs	Crucifix 10 Sets 8 Reps 80 lbs	Deltoid Shrugs 8 Sets 10 Reps 170 lbs	
Saturday's Cardiovascular Workout	Jumping Jacks 8 min	Shadow Wrestling 12 min	Sprints 20 min	Drilling Moves 30 min	
Sunday's Day of Rest and Relaxation					

Frequently Asked Questions

FREQUENTLY ASKED QUESTIONS

Where do you go to school?
I'm a sophomore at the University of Georgia, majoring in Broadcast News.

Can you use chopsticks?
No, but don't think I haven't tried.

How can you play video games?
I use my right foot to hit the trigger on an Xbox controller and my arms to manage the top buttons.

How do you eat spaghetti?
By twirling it up on a fork like anyone else.

Can you pump gas?
Only if there's a friend in the car to help.

What are your favorite movies?
Braveheart, Fight Club, Saving Private Ryan

What's your favorite song?
Eye of the Tiger by Survivor

Who's your favorite band/musician?
Chevelle, Tool, Linkin Park

Who are your favorite actors?
Jim Caviezel, Brad Pitt, Mel Gibson

Who are your favorite actresses?
Salma Hayek, Hilary Duff, Eva Mendes

What are your favorite books?
The Bible; Winning the Future; Dune

What's your favorite city?
Athens, GA

What are your favorite sports teams?
Atlanta Falcons and Atlanta Braves

Who are your top five favorite male athletes?
Andy Roddick, LaVar Arrington, Scott Stephens, Shaquille O'Neil, Dave Mirra

Who are your top five favorite female athletes?
Maria Sharapova, Amanda Weir, Mia Hamm, Michelle Wie, Cheri Blauwet

Who are your top five favorite combat athletes?
Muhammad Ali, Leila Ali, Randy Couture, Forrest Griffin, Cael Sanderson

What are your favorite sports (aside from grappling)?
Ultimate Fighting, Football, Tennis

What's your favorite color?
Turquoise

What's your favorite wrestling move?
Jap Whizzer

What's your favorite food?
Guacamole dip

What's your favorite drink?
Mountain Dew (though sweet tea's a very close second)

What's your favorite ice cream flavor?
Cookie Dough

What's your favorite game?
Texas Hold 'Em

What's your favorite TV show?
SportsCenter

What's your favorite pizza topping?
Sausage and Mushrooms

What are your major long term goals?
Graduate from the University of Georgia with a degree in Broadcast News, do as many public speeches as I can to spread the *No Excuses* message, eventually open a chain of wellness centers centered the *No Excuses* attitude, and coach a wrestling team of my own.

What's one of your short term goals?
Win my next match.